INDEBTED AMERICA

Daniel Patrick Brown

LUX ET SAPIENTIA

Albrecht

For inquiries, please contact:
customerservice.albrecht@yahoo.com

Published 2025 by Albrecht

21 20 19 18 1 2 3 4

ISBN 979-8-218-86999-1
ISBN 978-1-7321088-9-9 ebook

For

Earl Frederick Brown, DVM
Katharine Appleby "Kay" Brown
and
Michael A. Brown

Also by Daniel Patrick Brown

American Chronicle:
An Inclusive History (Volume I)

Enduring Entanglements:
The Third Reich's Insidious Impact on America

The Beautiful Beast:
The Life & Crimes of SS-Aufseherin Irma Grese

The Camp Women:
The Female SS Auxiliaries Who Served in the
Nazi Concentration Camps

The Protectorate and the Northumberland Conspiracy:
Political Intrigue in the Reign of Edward VI

The Tragedy of Libby and Andersonville Prison Camps:
A Study of Mismanagement and Inept Logistical Policies at Two
Southern Prisoner-of-War Camps during the Civil War

Woodrow Wilson and the Treaty of Versailles:
The German Leftist Press' Response

CONTENTS

Part I: The Origin and Evolution of Indebted America

Part II: Indebted America in the Modern Age

Part III: Remedies for American Indebtedness

Part I: The Origin and Evolution of Indebted America

CHAPTER 1

THE CURRENT INDEBTEDNESS
OF AMERICANS

We have met the enemy and he is us.

—Pogo, the opossum character in Wal Kelly's
cartoon strip of the same name

IN THE FIRST QUARTER of 2025, millions of Americans find themselves deeply in debt due to the high balances that they have on their credit cards. Nationally, credit card debt is approaching $1.7 trillion and according to the latest report from the Federal Reserve Bank of Philadelphia, average individual credit card balances at the end of 2024 hit their highest levels in twelve years. Nearly eleven percent of American card holders are making only the requisite minimum payment monthly on their cards and approximately 3.5% of all balances are at least thirty days past due.

According to Lending Tree, to make matters even more dire for those behind on repaying their credit card debts, the average interest rate on a credit card right now is 24.25%. Although the inflation rate has come down somewhat, prices now are still higher than they were five years ago. What is more troubling is that most groceries, which are essential expenditures, are twenty-eight percent more expensive than in 2020. The Federal Reserve Bank reports that more consumers are using their credit cards to live. Moreover, when one adds in the dramatic rise in fixed home mortgage interest rates, many Americans will be tied to their long-term financial obligation for years and, *for some, many more decades*, to come.[1]

In terms of the United States' national indebtedness, as of March 2025, America has both the world's biggest national debt, which resolves to a debt-to-GDP ratio of approximately 121.31% (the per capita rate is a staggering $98,204).[2] U.S. spending so far for FY 2025 (July 1, 2024–June 30, 2025) has been $711 billion, which is $201 billion more than the same period in the previous fiscal year. The Peter G. Peterson Foundation, a nonpartisan organization dedicated to increasing ". . . public awareness of the nature and urgency of the key fiscal challenges threatening America's future and to accelerate action on them," warns Americans that the nation's out of control spending must be addressed. It has stated that

> Fiscal year 2025 has gotten off to a bad start in terms of growth in the deficit. The federal debt is approaching its post-World War II high and is on track to continue rising rapidly, which is unsustainable. The new Administration and Congress must take action to put the nation on a more sustainable footing.[3]

Clearly, a large portion of Americans are deeply in debt, but the federal government is hardly setting a good example itself.

CHAPTER 2

INDENTURED SERVITUDE IN EXCHANGE FOR A VOYAGE TO THE NEW WORLD

It's you. The indentured servant. I mean,
the tenant-slash-cleaning lady.

—Celeste Ng,
Little Fires Everywhere (2017)

AMERICANS HAVE HAD A long and often tortured history with debt. Indeed, from America's inception, many of
its earliest inhabitants from Europe had to go into debt just to
face the challenges of trying to make it to the New World. Today,
few Americans seldom consider—or simply don't realize—just
how oppressive, and occasionally intolerable, life was for those
born into the lower classes in Europe at the time of the New
World's alleged "discovery," (the reality was that Indigenous people had already "discovered" the Western Hemisphere). Often,
only after a contemporary American reads one of Charles Dickens'
or Victor Hugo's novels, does he/she have an inkling of just how
brutally repressive the class system was in most of Europe. For
those low-born, working-class people, a lifetime of hopeless
drudgery was the only existence that was possible in their native
European lands. For these "miserable ones," to borrow Hugo's

term, the single hope for them was to try to escape their plight by somehow getting to the new lands of opportunity across the Atlantic Ocean.

The sole solution for most of them was to barter with a bonds-man for the costly passage to the New World. In exchange for their transatlantic voyage, these destitute men and women would forfeit their freedom and submit to hard labor for a set amount of time in the New World to repay their debt. They were classified as bonded or indentured servants and their commitments to serve their masters generally existed somewhere between five and seven years. Most of these male indentured servants worked as farm laborers and most of the women served as domestic servants. These debtors often worked in deplorable conditions, were exposed to the elements, and were given the bare necessities to survive. If they completed their bonded indentureship, those hearty souls who endured their ordeal could potentially live as free people in a classless society. The sad reality was that of all the northern and western European newcomers, *roughly fifty to seventy-five* percent who came to the colonies between the 1630s and the start of the American War of Independence came as indentured servants.[4]

Obviously, debt in this instance was simply something that most of America's earliest inhabitants had to request. This commitment is nothing that those Euromericans should feel ashamed about; indeed, in this instance, their decision to go into debt to obtain a better life for themselves and their children is something to be honored and celebrated. In addition, many creditworthy Americans have been rendered insolvent at various times in U.S. history due to panics, recessions, and depressions. Although some of these eras were triggered by the inevitable dips in the business cycle, others, such as the Panic of 1837, were due to political and business leaders' decisions. In this case, the economic meltdown did not occur until shortly after President Andrew Jackson left office. However, the panic was caused by Jackson's decisions—not his successor's, Martin Van Buren, who was unfairly blamed for it and then degraded as "Martin Van *Ruin*."[5]

Those Europeans who were able to come to the New World without going into debt sometimes benefited from war or due to a nation wanting to expand its influence in the New World. For example, following the suppression of the Monmouth Rebellion of 1685, Lord Justice George Jeffreys, 1st Baron Jeffreys, PC (known as "the Hanging Judge") and his "Bloody Assizes" (trials) sentenced almost seven percent of the rebels to death. In a strange twist of fate, those lucky enough to be exiled ultimately lived better by virtue of getting to the North American colonies in chains but free from having to go into debt. In another instance, a prison reforming member of Parliament, James George Oglethorpe, was able to get the last of the thirteen colonies, Georgia, established with land ceded to it from the colony of South Carolina. He was able to get it founded as a refuge for the insolvent British adults languishing in debtors' prisons. Although the initial inhabitants of the new colony were not former prisoners, in time, thousands of debtors were brought to the crown colony. Every debtor received fifty acres of arbitrarily designated plots, which they were obligated to make fruitful and subsist on with the proviso included that this gift was not to be sold. Unfortunately, many of these areas were not suitable for northern crops. Oglethorpe's grand experiment failed because large numbers of supposedly reformed debtors abandoned their barren lands and simply crossed over into adjoining colonies. Finally, "Henry" Astor (born *Johann Heinrich Astor*), the brother of America's first millionaire, "John" Astor ((born *Johann Jakob Astor*), signed on to become one of the "Hessian" mercenaries who fought for the British in the American colonies during the War of Independence. Henry deserted his unit once he was in America, opened his own butcher shop in Manhattan, and then stole cattle from farmers in the outlying countryside to slaughter and sell the meat at a one percent profit.[6]

When the Declaration of Independence was finalized and fifty-six American colonial representatives affixed their signatures to the document, two—James Wilson and Robert Morris—had been incarcerated in debtors' prisons and one, Button Gwinnett, had had a long history of borrowing money and then fleeing from financial accountability. Gwinnett, a delegate from Georgia, was born in England, borrowed the funds for his transatlantic passage to the colonies, and never repaid the debt. Then, he borrowed money to make a fresh start as a merchant in Charleston, South Carolina, but that failed and, again, he did not repay his debt. Yet again, Gwinnett borrowed money to start a business in Savannah and when it languished, he simply walked away from his financial obligation. Following this, he then thought he could become a plantation owner, so Gwinnett obtained a loan, bought slaves as well as St. Catherine's Island off the coast of Georgia. Once again, his venture failed and the creditors took the island and the slaves and, yet again, Gwinnett walked away from his debt and his family was left nothing but its home. There is no record that Gwinnett ever repaid any of these debts.[7] While most of the signatories to the Declaration of Independence were honorable men, the unscrupulous behavior of Gwinnett must also be acknowledged.

Following America's independence, the states instituted the Articles of Confederation on March 1, 1781. Fearful of allowing another tyranny to establish itself, the states prohibited the inclusion of an executive branch, and the thirteen independent and semi-autonomous states did not consider themselves a part of an amalgamized nation; rather, the governmental apparatus simply recognized the *United* States as a league of friendship—a loose assemblage of associated states. Why is it important to add this component to an examination of American indebtedness? This matter is relevant because the Articles of Confederation did not provide the states with the power to regulate the economy in all states, impose taxes nationwide, or fund a national defense. Everything came to a head in 1786-1787 when Captain Daniel Shays led a mob of about one thousand disgruntled, debt-ridden western Massachusetts farmers to revolt against their pending foreclosures. Consequently, it was clear that the nascent republic needed to either reform or replace its current form of government.

CHAPTER 3

THE BANKRUPTCY OPTION

Capitalism without bankruptcy is like Christianity without hell.

—Frank Borman, former U.S. Astronaut
and CEO of Eastern Airlines

THE CONSTITUTIONAL CONVENTION OF 1787 ultimately solved the economic crisis. Although the creation of the U.S. Constitution scrapped the previous inept system and an executive branch was included as one of the key additions, the delegates to the Constitutional Convention infused integral fail-safe provisions to prevent tyranny from arising from within the new governmental infrastructure. In addition, the "Bankruptcy Code" (Article I, Section 8, Clause 4) was included to provide the fledgling nation's hundreds of thousands of debtors with a mechanism to reconcile their financial obligations.

One detrimental side effect of America's new bankruptcy code was that ". . . even as they came and went again, made taking risks less risky for everyone, which meant that everyone took more risks."[8]

Due to many factors, none the least of which was an ever-changing economy coupled with international commercial fluctuations, Congress has had to periodically generate new bankruptcy acts. The 1800 version, which had provided for involuntary bankruptcy, was repealed in 1803 due to ". . . its ineffectiveness, abuse of its provisions, and the awkwardness of dealing the nascent federal court system."[9]

Native Americans were not immune to the ever-lurking danger of economic insolvency. The highly indebted Choctaw people elected to sell their land to the U.S. government in exchange ". . . for the sum of six thousand dollars, annually, forever."[10]

Chapter 4

Indebted Presidents, Vice Presidents, and Prominent Americans

Never spend your money before you have earned it.

—Thomas Jefferson,
the Third President of the United States

I F ANY CONTINGENT OF U.S. citizens might be free of debt, one would think that those who served as the nation's chief executives would surely be the one. After all, these individuals have generally aspired to lead by example. However, only a few presidents, particularly those who served prior to the last quarter of the nineteenth century, died free of debt. For one thing, they would only receive a $25,000 annual salary until Grant's second term in 1873, when it was doubled to $50,000 a year. Secondly, they had to pay for many of their job-related expenses out of their own pockets.

The "Father of the Country" himself, George Washington, was indebted for a short period in the 1760s when his tobacco farm went bankrupt. Indeed, America's first president had to secure a loan just so he could travel to New York City to be sworn in as president for the first time. Nonetheless, he was a proud man who refused his annual salary when he first assumed office. In the end, Washington's agricultural operations put him back in the black and he did not die insolvent.

Thomas Jefferson was one of the first Americans to take advantage of the first U.S. bankruptcy option. Despite Jefferson's advice to "never spend your money before you have earned it," he enjoyed more lavish, sometimes extravagant, amenities than he could afford. Even after selling off many of his beloved books in 1815, Jefferson died in the red to the tune of $107,000, or roughly the equivalent of two million dollars in today's currency.[11]

James Madison, like Washington and Jefferson before him, was so short of cash that when he bought a multitude of books in Philadelphia before returning to his estate at Montpelier, he had to sell off some property to compensate for the book purchases. He attempted to sell his personal slave, "Billey," whom he had owned from his birth in 1759 (Madison himself had been eight years old at the time), Madison discovered that he could not sell Billey even if he wanted to because he was in Pennsylvania and a 1780 abolition law in that state prevented any such transaction. Nonetheless, Madison eventually sold Billey as an indentured servant, thereby limiting his servitude to seven years. While Madsion found it necessary to sell his household slave to get himself out of debt, this transaction provided Billey, who renamed himself William Gardener, the rare opportunity to escape slavery.

James Monroe, the sixth American president, was reckless with his income and found himself deeply mired in debt when he left office in 1825. While it is true that, like his predecessors, he had to cover most of his expenses when he served on diplomatic missions to Europe, a large portion of his debt was due to his own mismanagement. He had no compunction in asking Congress to reimburse him $29,513, which the legislative branch approved in 1826. Still, Monroe's debt was so high that he filed additional claims and received another $30,000 in 1831 (the total of the two congressional compensation packages, $59,513 was approximately the equivalent a million dollars today). For his estate's benefit, following his death, Congress appropriated even additional funds to secure his papers from his heirs.[12]

Building on his military success, America's ninth president, William Henry Harrison was appointed the U.S. ambassador to Colombia prior to being elected president and spent a year abroad. During this period, his debt only increased. When he returned home, his family farm had lost its crops in bad weather and Harrison was pursued by creditors. By the time Harrison ascended to the White House in 1841, he was close to bankruptcy. He served as president for only thirty-two days after giving his inaugural address outside on a cold, blustery day in Washington, D.C. His speech was the longest in presidential history and he developed a cold that progressed into full-blown pneumonia that cost Harrison his life on April 4, 1841.

Millard Fillmore, the thirteenth president, was born into poverty and his father, Nathaniel, contracted his son to a clothmaker and Milliard fulfilled his seven-year commitment, paid a thirty-dollar fee, and was henceforth granted his freedom.

In 1832, several years before he became the sixteenth president, Abraham Lincoln opened a business with a friend. However, the business was unsuccessful, as it spent more than it took in, and after Lincoln's partner died, the future president decided to bear the brunt of the debt rather than saddle his friend's grieving family with any of the money owed to creditors.

Creditors went after Lincoln in court, and the sheriff took his only remaining assets: his horse and his surveying gear. He was effectively bankrupt before today's more generous bankruptcy laws were in place.[13]

Andrew Johnson, Lincoln's successor and America's seventeenth president, was "apprenticed" with his brother, William, by his mother, Mary, to a tailor. After enduring the drudgery of such unpaid labor for a couple years, Andrew and William Johnson simply did what some other bond[ed] servants had done before: they saw an opportunity to escape and fled. Despite the efforts of the tailor to hunt them down, they were ever apprehended.

America's eighteenth president, Ulysses S. Grant, he invested in a financial firm that his son, Ulysses S. "Buck" Grant Jr., thought would be profitable; however, when a third investor embezzled the funds, the business failed, and Grant went bankrupt along with his son. To become solvent once again, the former president wrote his memoir focused on his experiences in the Civil War and it became a best-seller. His family was left with $450,000 in royalties, which would be more than eleven million dollars in today's currency. Grant did not live to see his economic turnaround, as he was dying of throat cancer and struggled to survive just long enough to complete his memoir.[14]

James A. Garfield, the twentieth U.S. president, competes with Milliard Fillmore and Andrew Johnson as the poorest man ever to become president. Garfield was born in a log cabin, and his father died when the future president was still a toddler. Consequently, his family was relegated to abject poverty. The resourceful young Garfield worked on canal boats, as a janitor, and as a carpenter to pay his family's debts and due to his hard work and frugal disposition, he was eventually able to free his family from insolvency. At the same time, he read and studied in preparation for going to college.

Garfield would become a professor, a lawyer, a minister, a Civil War hero, and finally the president of the United States. Though he achieved the highest office in the land, Garfield still had very little money to his name when his life was cut short by an assassin's bullet in 1881.

The twenty-fifth U.S. president, William McKinley, was financially ruined in 1893 when he co-signed loans for a friend (who ultimately defaulted and left McKinley insolvent). Thanks to wealthy friends, McKinley's debts were paid. When he was assassinated in 1901, McKinley was solvent; however, he was not wealthy.

Harry Truman, who became America's thirty-third president upon the death of Franklin Delano Roosevelt in April 1945, was a serial entrepreneur who failed at many economic ventures prior to becoming FDR's running mate in 1944. He began his professional life in banking and was an effective bank teller, but then his father, who had been wiped out financially, needed Harry to work on the farm that his mother inherited from her wealthy brother. Truman hated farming, but he threw himself into being a good farmer, in part by educating himself about crop rotation and learning how to handle horses. Nevertheless, the Trumans never earned enough money to offset the large mortgages on their farmlands and despite farming for a decade, Harry acknowledged that, "he never made a dime doing it." Truman had invested heavily in a lead and zinc firm in Oklahoma that failed and the haberdashery business he co-owned also faltered.[15] When President Truman entered the White House, he was still indebted. However, he refused to declare bankruptcy on moral grounds, but even his $75,000 presidential salary was not enough to free him from debt.[16] Interestingly, Harry Truman was only able to regain solvency in 1955 when his family farm in Grandview, Missouri, was developed into a shopping center, which was named, "the Truman Corners Town and Country Shoppers City."

Vice-presidents also struggled with indebtedness. Aaron Burr, America's third vice president, has been derided since he mortally wounded Alexander Hamilton in an 1804 duel. There is no question that Burr had his flaws and his blatant attempt to seize land in the West cannot be ignored. In addition, Jefferson's vice-president pursued speculative real estate ventures, which landed him in debt and would keep him moving to avoid creditors for more than three decades. It is important to note that his situation was not unique: Jefferson, Hamilton, and Monroe were all debtors. In the case of Hamilton, both he and Burr owed money to the same man, Ezra Weeks, a major builder in New York. Also, both Hamilton and Burr served as counsel in defending Ezra's brother, Levi, in the murder of a young Quaker lady named Gulielma Sands. While none of the founders were ever committed to a debtors' prison, without their power and prestige, some would have very possibly have been incarcerated. Unfortunately for Burr, his only option was to keep ahead of his creditors by moving a great deal and, in 1808, this entailed crossing the Atlantic Ocean to Great Britain. Burr returned in 1812 and established a law office under his mother's maiden name (Edwards) to continue to foil his creditors' efforts to recoup their losses.[17]

Elbridge Gerry, the fifth vice-president, lived well beyond his means and became almost completely bankrupt. When he died, his family was left destitute. Congress ultimately had to allocate money to pay for the vice president's burial.[18]

Finally, America's thirty-seventh vice-president and following John F. Kennedy's assassination, the thirty-sixth U.S. president, Lyndon Baines Johnson, grew up in a similar situation to Truman—he experienced poverty first-hand because what small amount of money his father possessed was taken when LBJ was a young man. What ultimately brought President Johnson out of indebtedness was his marriage to Claudia "Lady Bird" Taylor. Her shrewd investments in a Texas-based radio and television station allowed LBJ to make himself solvent and afforded him the opportunity to pursue political office.[19]

If American chief executives and their vice presidents were indebted, imagine how many others were as well. Even well-known individuals struggled with debt their entire lives. For example, two nineteenth century contemporaries, David Crockett and Edgar A. Poe (neither of whom preferred to be known as "Davy" Crockett or Edgar "Allen" Poe), were never able to rise above poverty and indebtedness. In fairness to both Crockett, Poe, and thousands of other Americans living in the first half of the nineteenth century, there had been two major global downturns in the economy, the Panic of 1819 and the Panic of 1837. The 1837 depression, which was partially caused by the overextension of credit, was the worst American economic crisis until the Great Depression of 1929 and it lasted for seven years (the decade of the 1840s became widely known as "the Hungry Forties").[20]

In David Crockett's case, he grew up in abject poverty—sometimes the family bordered on being downright destitute; in fact, before David even reached adolescence, his father, John, had to "bind out," essentially a form of indentured servitude, his son to a stock herder just to pay off one of his many debts. Nonetheless,

David Crockett never complained about his "lot in life." He stated in his autobiography that his father simply had "neither the means nor the opportunity" to provide him or any of his siblings with an education, much less a place at the family table.[21]

To illustrate just how bad things became for Edgar A. Poe, his motivation for writing his 1843 short story *The Gold-Bug* was to stave off starvation; indeed, he had been so poor that he had to subsist for long periods of time by only consuming bread and molasses.[22] In June 1842, a destitute Poe wrote that "my only hope of relief is the Bankruptcy Act." While Congress passed the Bankruptcy Act of 1841 to help alleviate the accumulated insolvent debt, swindlers quickly found loopholes in this effort and then began to game the system. In turn, Congress immediately retracted the Act.[23] In the end, even the passage of the 1841 version of the bankruptcy code was of no benefit to him and he died eight years later still destitute.

CHAPTER 5

THE AMERICAN MARKET REVOLUTION

*Economic progress emerges from the intelligent
combination of capital and innovation.*

—Yaron Brook,
In Pursuit of Wealth (2017)

BETWEEN THE 1820S AND 1850s, the United States witnessed a dramatic transition from the rudimentary labor system in the South, spurred on in part by Eli Whitney's development of the cotton gin, that made the economy more efficient with increased production of many goods. This innovative period in business made its way to the North. Accompanying this transition was the improvement of transportation. Appropriately called the Market Revolution, the improvements and innovations in business would continue into the early twentieth century. The growth and development of new manufacturing techniques and processes ameliorated domestic productivity and made the United States less reliant on foreign trade while economic exchange within America increased. At the same time, the greater demand for cotton internationally helped fuel the Southern economy, which conspicuously benefited the slaveholders, but also enriched many textile factory owners in New England. This boom would also encourage American leaders to acquire more lands "out west," which, naturally, only increased violent confrontations with Native Americans and Mexicans for ownership of their lands.[24] Indeed, to measure just how dramatic this shift had become vis-à-vis the Old World (Europe), by 1890, American manufacturing production had eclipsed both Great Britain and Germany combined.[25]

One important development of the Market Revolution was it allowed the United States to be less reliant on foreign trade while economic exchange within the country simultaneously increased. This amazing economic transformation could not have occurred without the advent of credit. While many colonial Americans had been debtors, it was not until the Market Revolution period that credit would become critical for the economy's growth and, as a result, it expanded. Moreover, the interlocking credit obligations between so many different lenders and borrowers facilitated U.S. territorial expansion.[26]

CHAPTER 6

FOREIGN OBSERVERS' VIEWS
OF AMERICAN BANKRUPTCY

Bankruptcy represents a longstanding commitment in this country to helping people get a fresh start. This principle has never been [about] *giving only certain people a fresh start.*

—Senator Tim Johnson (D-SD), former chairman
of the Senate Banking Committee

IN THE EARLY 1820S, Francis J. Grund, an Austrian immigrant, observed that, "there is, probably, no other country in which credit is so purely personal as in the United States." Grund's impressions of Americans and their preoccupation with obtaining credit were published in his 1837 book *The Americans.* Grund was fascinated with the level of trust that Americans placed in one another when extending credit. Since Grund came from a class-based culture that held firm to its Old-World prejudices, he marveled that a socioeconomic environment could exist in which monetary trust was so accessible. To the Austrian math and language educator, the easy extension of credit was something bold and beneficial to the emerging nation.[27]

Another tourist, Alexis de Tocqueville, whose actual title was Charles Henri Clérel, comte de Tocqueville, was a French aristocrat and civil servant who traveled extensively throughout the United States from July 1831 to February 1832 on a mission to examine American prisons and penitentiaries on behalf of the French government. He is best known for his *Democracy in America*, which was published in two volumes in 1835 and 1840. De Tocqueville's insights and observations about the nascent nation fascinated Europeans and instilled pride in many Americans that an astute European would speak highly of their grand experiment, particularly concerning constitutional components like the power of judicial review—a legal device that no European could fathom at that time.[28]

De Tocqueville questioned why bankruptcy was permitted ". . . so remarkedly indulgent toward businessmen who go bankrupt. An accident of this sort leaves no stain on his honor. In this respect, Americans are different not only from the peoples of Europe but from all other modern trading nations."[29] Nevertheless, as previously noted, while new bankruptcy laws have been abused by devious and self-serving individuals, bedeviled by ineffective provisions, and/or cumbersome and convoluted provisions in the new codes, without such financial relief for honorable people hopelessly indebted due to such occurrences as catastrophic medical emergencies, they could be potentially condemned to a life of misery.

Chapter 7

Gold, Gilding, and Easier Access to Credit

Our frustration is greater when we have much and want more than when we have nothing and want some.

—Eric Hoffer, *The True Believer*, Chapter V
("The Poor"), Section 23, pp. 29-30

JOHANN AUGUST SUTER, WHO Anglicized his name to "John Sutter," was born in the German-speaking portion of the Holy Roman Empire. He attempted to make a living as an entrepreneur, but a series of financial failures in Switzerland drove him into bankruptcy. Sutter promptly abandoned his wife and children and migrated to northern California in 1839. Sutter worked with the Mexican authorities to establish the colony of *Nueva Helvetia* (New Switzerland); however, when gold was discovered on his land, Sutter was not able to benefit from the discovery because the Treaty of Guadalupe Hidalgo, which resulted in the United States obtaining a huge expanse of the southwestern territories, now voided his arrangement with Mexico. Moreover, as prospectors overran Sutter's land, they stole and destroyed his goods and livestock. Sutter would petition the U.S. courts for compensation for his losses, but his efforts were futile. By 1852, he was once again bankrupt.[30]

Following the Civil War, Americans found themselves contending with a weakened economy. It was truly heartbreaking, but approximately thirteen percent of white children and thirty percent of black children were left with only a female parent to guide them. To make matters worse, there were large numbers of orphans—some institutionalized and some trying to survive on the streets—for society to contend with. Those surviving on the streets only by their wits were frequently depicted in the press and literature as "waifs and strays," "street urchins," and so forth. This led a young aspiring novelist, Horatio Alger, who had become obsessed by the homeless boys he passed by in New York City, to feature them as his models in fulfilling the American dream.[31] With the publication of his "dime novel," a *Bildungsroman* or a sort of "coming-of-age" writing, *Ragged Dick; or, Street Life in New York with the Boot Blacks*, Alger touched the public's nerve and the diminutive writer was able to capitalize on a largely untapped audience—downtrodden young American boys hoping for success in the seemingly hopeless world of the "haves and the have nots." While most of these young people barely sustained themselves in horrible conditions and near starvation, there were a miniscule number who were able to elevate themselves to a modest existence.

To address the debilitated business environment, Congress passed the Bankruptcy Act of 1867, which was more lenient to debtors than the 1841 version. The goal was to allow creditors who were owed $250.00 or more or those indebted by at least $300.00 to discharge their financial liabilities. It is a sad statement of fact, but former slaveholders benefited from the passage of the new bankruptcy act. Although Southerners comprised only a quarter of the U.S. population, they possessed most of the debt in 1867 and they were responsible for thirty-six percent off all the bankruptcy applications; consequently, this new provision provided them with the opportunity to secure their land and protect their assets.[32]

Unfortunately, the United States simultaneously entered the Reconstruction Era, the Gilded Age[33], and the Victorian Age. It was during this period that cartels, trusts, and syndicates were set up by business moguls to artificially fix prices and, in certain instances, manufacture scarcity. Likewise, political corruption increased while class warfare accelerated. Because the markets experienced wild economic swings, "stock market frenzies, panics, and crashes" primed instability and this made the lives of so many Americans even more difficult. When Ulysses S. Grant began his second term as president, the economy fell into a depression. In January 1873, Congress passed the Coinage Act (also known as the Mint Act). The major shift in monetary policy demonetized silver, which terminated American bimetallism and concurrently halted the coinage of silver dollars. From that point onward, the U.S. Treasury would only allow for the trade of silver with those countries that were still on the silver standard, such as China. Denounced by silver adherents as the "Crime of '73," the big losers were the silver miners, principally in Nevada, who had struck silver bonanzas in the 1860s and '70s. On September 8th, banks began to fold and ten days later the banking firm of Jay Cooke & Company, which both the president and his minister to France, Elihu Washburne, had invested in, also closed its doors. Cooke's bank, like many others, had been heavily invested in railroad construction. The economic collapse forced Wall Street to suspend trading for ten days. The sudden downturn was a shock and Grant's economic advisors did little to alleviate the economic crisis, but this was a pre-regulatory era in which the national government could not do much to halt the downturn. The crisis only deepened, and it would drag on through the entire second term of Grant's administration and the first two years that Rutherford Birchard Hayes was president. In 1878, the new effort to provide relief largely failed and the Bankruptcy Act of 1867 was repealed.[34]

What exacerbated economic instability further was the advent of self-serving speculative investors and ruthless businessmen—such as J. P. Morgan, John D. Rockefeller, Jay Gould, and others—who were able to operate in the grey areas of American jurisprudence while concurrently understanding that the lack of regulatory oversight afforded them room to manipulate and exploit "the system." The net effect was that the disparity between such ultrarich "Robber Barons," or more benignly designated "Captains of Industry," and the masses of blue-collar workers, both industrial as well as agricultural, grew dramatically. In fact, by 1870, the richest one percent of the U.S. population controlled over twenty-five percent of America's wealth. Even after concerted efforts by Populists and Progressives in the late nineteenth/early twentieth centuries to redistribute some of the excess affluence of the "one per-centers," the maldistribution became more pronounced: some estimates claim that by the eve of the Great War, ten percent of the U.S. population controlled ninety percent of its wealth. According to "The State of U.S. Wealth Inequality," today the top ten percent of Americans possess sixty-seven percent of all the U.S. household wealth.[35]

Mark Twain, the *nom de plume* of American humorist and essayist Samuel Langhorne Clemens, bemoaned the impact that the Robber Barons had on American society. He observed that there had been respected men of means before the late nineteenth century, but the current crop of financial and industrial magnates, ". . . taught the entire nation to make a god of the money and the man, no matter how money might have been acquired."

Mark Twain was yet another American who struggled most of his life handling money. He not only squandered his massive wealth from book royalties, but he also lost a substantial amount of his wife's inheritance. Twain's predilection to get involved with foolhardy business schemes ultimately necessitated the Twain family to go into a nine-year exile overseas to avoid creditors and alleviate the strain of his bankruptcy.[36]

The genesis of the modern debt economy began in 1878 at Frank Mackey's jewelry store in Minneapolis, Minnesota. When Mackey received a sizeable inheritance, he redesigned his jewelry store into a makeshift loan office to provide "settlers from both the East and from Europe" funds to allow them "make it" as settlers in the Dakota territories. Mackey's model became a success, and he named his new enterprise the "Household Finance Corporation."[37]

By the 1920s, HFC had expanded its operation throughout the United States to establish itself as the epicenter of the subprime lenders. These are individuals willing to make loan arrangements for high-risk borrowers due to their lack of collateral or established credit history. In truth, however, Mackey's company simply represents a long thread in American debt. His original jewelry shop was always an operational pawnshop that served its desperate clients more and John Mackey was simply a loan shark who could legally forego the old usury prohibitions, that is, the biblical condemnation of making loans that are unfairly enriching the lender because the borrower is charged an excessively high interest rate. For those unfortunate lower-wage earners, when a major financial crisis arose, they invariably had no choice but to go to an HFC office to secure an exploitive loan.

Mackey did not go unchallenged for charging these exorbitant interest rates on his loans. In 1885, he incurred four lawsuits for loans that had provided him with 300 percent profit margins. Although lower courts sided with Mackey, Minnesota's Supreme Court found his loans to be usurious, and he was fined. Undeterred, Mackey wrote the fines off as business expenses and over the next two decades expanded his operation across other states.[38]

By 1895, HFC became the first American financial company to offer installment plans to its borrowers. However, the first installment plans were secured (collateralized), which required the borrower to commit a valuable item as security for repayment of a loan. If the borrower defaulted on the loan, then the lender would take possession of the collateralized object. One major advantage to those who were able to secure collateralized loans was that the interest rate charged by the lending institution was usually lower than non-collateralized loans.

The terms of these consumer loans ostensibly benefited the consumer because he/she did not have to make a lump sum payment to pay off the balance and, therefore, it provided the borrower with the opportunity to remit payments via more modest monthly amounts. However, even if the borrower followed the payment schedule and paid off the loan in full, because the loan took longer to mature, the interest on the loan would increase and, for the mere chance to have this extended time, more money would be paid by the consumer than had it been paid sooner. In addition, if the monthly payments are extended over many years, one personal monetary hardship (such as the loss of one's job, a medical emergency, and so forth) could result in the forfeiture of the collateral as well as whatever product the borrower had signed on for. Still, for those who had no savings to rely on in the event of an economic calamity, quite often they had little choice but to borrow.

American political economic historian Louis R. Hyman's research reveals that HFC could rightly claim that the company saved many clients from complete insolvency. Also, Hyman has shown that while the overwhelming majority of HFC's loans were made to people from the working-class, there were often irresponsible borrowers who came from the professions as well.[39]

CHAPTER 8

THE RISE OF NEW LABOR-SAVING DEVICES AS WELL AS DEPARTMENT STORES

If we want anything, all we have to do is to go and buy it on credit, so that leaves us without any economic problem whatever, except perhaps someday to have to pay them [sic].

—Will Rogers, quoted in Watts, *Citizen Cowboy*, p.159

THE TERM "YANKEE INGENUITY" began to be used in newspapers and broadsheets in the early years of the American republic. While the originator of the phrase is unknown, the expression was apropos due to the seemingly endless inventions and innovations created in the United States at the end of the eighteenth and start of the nineteenth centuries. Numerous devices and appliances became available. Some of the most significant inventions and adaptations were:

- in the effort to solve transportation problems with limited resources, the construction of the Erie Canal, which was completed in 1825, constituted an important engineering advancement toward America's westward expansion.

- In 1847, Samuel Finley Breese Morse's invention of the electric telegraph led to America's predominance in worldwide communication.

- Elias Howe received a patent in 1851 for his "Automatic, Continuous Clothing Closure," the prototype of what is today known as the sewing machine, an invention that allowed the garment industry to greatly increase the manufacture of inexpensive clothing.

- The "United Society of Believers in Christ's Second Appearing," a religious utopian community more commonly known as "the Shakers," took what they had learned about cleaning soiled clothing and employing mechanical power to produce a commercially viable washing machine in 1858. What set the Shakers' invention apart from other prototypes was that they augmented their device with a box mangle for pressing cloth as well as developing a specially formulated laundry soap to upgrade the cleanliness of the washed clothes.

- The "type-writer" or "mechanical writing machine" was patented in 1868 and this allowed trained operators to transcribe information twice as quickly as it could previously be written. In addition, the new device provided businesses with lucid correspondence and documentation.

- Thanks to the efforts of Alexander Graham Bell, Elisha Gray, and/or Antonio Meucci,[40] the telephone was created in 1876.

- In 1879, Thomas Edison and his team created a reliable, durable incandescent light bulb. Equally important, Edison also invented the system needed to bring electricity into homes, including dynamos, wires, fuses, and switches.

These inventions, among many others, provided Americans with better and often more efficient ways of getting things done. Mark Twain stated in an 1890 speech entitled, "On Foreign Critics," that "we are called the nation of inventors. And we are. We could still claim that title and wear its loftiest honors if we had stopped with the first thing we ever invented, which was human liberty."[41] In response to all these improvements, American consumer capitalism brought forth a culture that was virtually hostile to the past and to tradition. This new attitude fostered the belief that the best way to live was to enjoy all the new products and innovations that afforded Americans with the good life.[42]

At the same time all these inventions and amazing engineering feats manifestly advanced American society, department stores, uniquely self-contained businesses where consumers could go to buy virtually everything they needed in one location, began to spout up in the major eastern cities. Although the first department store, Arnold Constable, was founded in 1825 in New York City, it was not until the early twentieth century that department stores began to proliferate in multiple cities in the eastern half of the country. Marshall Field's (1902 and 1912) and Carson, Pirie, Scott and Company (1903) in Chicago, Macy's (1902) in Manhattan, Filene's (1912) in Boston, the white Famous-Barr (1913) in St. Louis, and the Lazarus store (1913) was torn down and rebuilt as a block-long store in Cincinnati.[43] Just as the industrial magnates like John D. Rockefeller, Andrew Carnegie, et al., had waged war with one another in the late nineteenth century, department store tycoons also began to engage in cut-throat competition for dominance in their economic spheres.

Social reformers like Edward Bellamy, who's popular 1886 novel *Looking Backwards* had put the retail store at the center of his tale and whose Nationalist movement (a uniquely American form of socialism), openly assailed what he termed "particularism," that is, allowing for too much economic competition. What Bellamy advocated was the removal of those engaged in their self-interested takeovers and, instead, putting everything under the control of fair-minded supervisors. The result in Bellamy's utopian view would be an American system that leads the world to a peaceful environment where class conflicts, social strife, and sectarian differences would be quelled. This led Bellamy's adherents to petition their legislative representatives to provide every adult with a guaranteed annual income, so that average workers could access the same products as the affluent.[44] Bellamy's message resonated with the critics of the Gilded Age and were reaffirmed in some of the values that Henry George's *Progress and Poverty* championed in his 1879 work, specifically that people should be able to reap the reward for what they produced themselves. George's equally socialistic perspective was that the economic value of land—including its natural resources—should belong equally to all members of society.

At the same time, department stores dazzled the public and the owners sought numerous methods to entice customers in. The stores' spent large amounts to create show windows and "towers of glass"—dazzling displays in retail buildings that attracted so many, particularly during the Christmas season. By 1910, new assortments of lights and light colors and hues had appeared to provide greater nuances to displays. These new forms included gaslight, arc light, prismatic light (efficiently designated daylight), carbon-burning electrical light, light that emanated from tungsten filaments, floodlights, and spotlights. Furthermore, in their efforts to entice even more consumers into their stores, merchants added the latest inventions to provide prospective customers with seamless comfort and leisure. The new innovations included "revolving doors," elevators and escalators, and wider aisles. Department stores upgraded their interiors by replacing the old iron and plain wood surfaces with bronze embellishments and mahogany woodwork. Finally, another technique retailers used to attract more customers was to create the "bargain basement." Here those with meager means could buy marked-down goods and cheaper versions of the better-quality brands found on the upper floors.[45] When New York City's Abraham & Strauss opened its doors in 1919, it was able to lure customers to the United States' first fully air-conditioned department store.

A thought provoking and widely read book appeared at the end of the nineteenth century and it took direct aim at the crass materialism developing in the United States. Thorstein Veblen, a Stanford University professor, coined the phrase "conspicuous consumption" in his book, *The Theory of the Leisure Class*. Veblen contended that the proclivity of so many American consumers to frivolously wield their money to acquire luxury goods and services was misguided at best and downright destructive at worst. Moreover, Veblen believed that this large contingent of the American consumers, some with discretionary income but some without, was regressing American society by emulating feudal and monarchial states. In attempting to achieve higher status via public displays of wealth, people had become prisoners of their extravagant spending, all to either attain or maintain a given social status.[46]

CHAPTER 9

THE GROWTH OF THE CREDIT RATING INDUSTRY

No nation in the history of the world was ever sitting as pretty. If we want anything, all we have to do is go and buy it on credit.

—Will Rogers, quoted in Watts, *Citizen Cowboy*, p. 193

SINCE ADVANCING MORE CREDIT became a requisite component of America's economic growth, businesses had to ascertain who, exactly, would be the ideal candidates to merit getting credit. After all, "credit" is derived from the Latin *creditum*, meaning "something entrusted to another or a loan." Although those who had sufficient wealth to receive secured loans existed, extending loans to them alone would not be sufficient. Also, in this largely anonymous world, well-dressed, well-connected, and glib individuals frequently appeared to seek credit for bold, sure-to-succeed new business ventures. Many of these individuals were simply deft swindlers. As creditors have learned, such a display of wealth is no guarantor that the person who has the fortune will be forthright and repay what he/she owes. Indeed, one need look no further than to the corrupt attorney Roy Cohn or his protégée, the 45th and 47th president of the United States,

Donald Trump, both of whom have had the means but not the desire to remit what they owed. Whether out of indifference or arrogance, many extraordinarily opulent individuals have refused to pay their debts. Consequently, creditworthiness is not about if one can pay but more a matter of *will* he/she do so.[46]

On the other hand, occasionally the person who seemed to be insolvent due to his/her ragged attire and lack of proper credentials would often be conscientious, honor-bound customers. So, how could businesses go about identifying creditworthy clients?

Rating agencies seemed to be the solution, and these enterprises began to emerge as early as the 1840s. These early businesses that evaluated merchants were the predecessors of Dun & Bradstreet. For consumers, the first businesses that specifically valued their creditworthiness appeared in New York City around 1870. By 1890, these firms had proliferated and could be found in numerous municipalities from New York to San Francisco.

By the 1920s, the credit management industry had developed sophisticated systems for quickly evaluating the information they had collected and making this information available to authorized companies for a price. However, the price the American public has had to pay to obtain unsecured consumer loans has been great. Gradually, the credit monitoring and appraisal businesses had to garner support from federal and state governments to create methods of establishing accurate appraisals of individual consumers' creditworthiness. Eventually the invasive tenacles of these agencies were either unseen or, more often, simply accepted. To wary consumer advocates, what exists is a systematic, pervasive, invisible, and intrusive behemoth surveillance system.[47]

PART II: INDEBTED AMERICA IN THE MODERN AGE

CHAPTER 10

NEW PERSPECTIVES IN THE EARLY TWENTIETH CENTURY

Conspicuous consumption of valuable goods is a means of reputability to the gentleman of leisure.

—Thorstein Veblen,
The Theory of the Leisure Class, p. 57

AT THE TURN OF the twentieth century, new trends in thought began to sweep across America that complemented living for today and minimizing worrying about monetary issues. In his 1906 book, *On Pragmatism*, William James advocated people consider living pragmatically; that is, they should nurture "the habit of always seeing an alternative, if not taking the usual for granted . . . of imagining foreign states of mind" more in a more practical manner. He believed individuals should understand that they alone hold the answers as to whether they lived rich, gratifying lives. Moreover, to achieve this end, he emphasized a mind-world connection, a "stream of consciousness," that pervaded everyone's daily existence. Furthermore, human beings possess infinite possibilities by developing their own creative powers of constructive thinking. In turn, a 'Mind-Cure' movement began to sweep America. James had used the term 'New Thought' as a component of mind-cure movement," championing the idea of "live and let live." Mind-cure proponents promoted a belief that we had but one life to live and the real cure for all our physical ailments lay in positive thinking.[48]

Like pragmatists, another new group of American mind-cure devotees, the Theosophists, began to advocate their beliefs around this time. They argued that wisdom and guidance can be found almost anywhere. Some Theosophists, more than a few who were outright occultists, have been dismissed by many Americans because they believed that "spirits" of dead people are in their presence and that mediums who conduct séances can communicate with such spirits. Karma, which originated in ancient Sanskrit texts, affirms that any action, work, or deed, has its effect or consequences, is upheld by Theosophists, as is reincarnation.

Although Thorstein Veblen's first wife was a Theosophist, the author of the *Theory of the Leisure Class* found the mind-cure movement to be nonsense. As a vociferous critic of conspicuous consumption, he thought the idea that heralding commercial excess would have a deleterious effect on American society. Beyond this, Veblen's 1922 book, *Absentee Ownership*, mocked the credo that crass commercialism had somehow changed the old work mentality into a more productive form of "make-believe" culture.[49]

Simon Patten, an American economist and the chair of the Wharton School of Business at the University of Pennsylvania, stood in direct opposition to Veblen's stance. Patten argued in his 1909 work, *Product and Climax*, that "factory-made goods, the department stores, the new corporate monopolies, the installment buying, the nickelodeons, the amusement parks" were all indicative of the new social surplus and that eventually they would lead to a better humanity. The traditional institutions of churches, libraries, and schools, had advanced "prohibitory moral agencies" which only held humankind back.[50] Patten also dismissed pessimists, critics, and utopians (Henry George, Henry Demarest Lloyd, et al.) who claimed that America was declining in the same manner which Rome had.[51]

Still, Thorstein Veblen took a more dismal look at what all the new labor-saving devices were doing to the American culture. He stated that new sorts of destitutes were now appearing across the country, specifically those who were without automobiles, yachts, and Newport cottages. In time, what had been luxuries became necessities and those without were envious and bitter. Icons exulting the mind-cure mindset were mass produced. One was the "no worry" Billikens doll, which had been created by a young woman from Kansas City, Missouri. Another was a smiling Buddha figure that came in both feminine and male forms that championed "the God of things as the ought to be."[52]

Mind-cure also found its way into popular culture. In children's literature. Eleanor Porter, author of the *Pollyanna* books, and L. Frank Baum, a businessman and window trimmer by trade who authored of *The Wonderful Wizard of Oz* and its spinoffs, wrote from the mind-cure vantage point.

Baum's *The Wonderful Wizard of Oz* was more popular than *Pollyanna*. A great deal of his series on the mythical land of Oz was influenced by Theosophic teachings. Baum's interest in Theosophy no doubt was guided by his mother-in-law, Matilda Joslyn Gage. Gage had been a leader in the women's rights movement and coauthored *The History of Woman Suffrage*. She detested established religion. She was incensed that virtually every established faith had rejected the notion of giving women the right to vote and with Theosophy, Gage saw an opportunity to merge some form of faith together with scientific knowledge that would provide women with their ordained rights. Gage thought highly of Madame Blavatsky's 1877 book, *Isis Unveiled*, because of Blavatsky's admiration of the great religious goddess of pharaonic Egypt.[53]

L. Frank Baum also revered Blavatsky and conducted séances in his home. In 1890, Baum wrote that "the age of faith is sinking slowly into the past." He felt that it was now time for Americans to embrace a "new unfaith." Since Theosophy was seen as a permissive mind-cure way of dealing with life and he saw it as compatible with his world view. He wrote about the Hinduist component that stated people do not sin; consequently, there was no need to feel any guilt about it. He opposed Prohibition. When he gained wealth and fame, he lived lavishly and went into debt (Baum had intended to cease writing Oz stories after his 1910 publication of *The Emerald City of Oz*, his 6th in the series, but financial pressures prompted him to write and publish *The Patchwork Girl of Oz* three years later, with seven other Oz books to follow).

Baum disregard for the danger of going into debt was summed up in his editorial in 1890 that:

> . . . the good things of life are given to be used and that the "rainy day" theory of saving is a good one if it does not serve as an excuse for denying yourself comforts. Don't feel embarrassed about "having oranges" [note, at this time, oranges were

expensive] on the "breakfast table every morning,"
even if your salaries are too small to pay for them.
So what if some men might be "forced to borrow
a few dollars. Who will be the gainer when Death
calls him to the last account—the man who can
say "I have lived!" or the man who can say "I have
saved?" To gain all the meat from the nut of life is
the essence of wisdom. Therefore, eat, drink, and
be merry—tomorrow you die.'[54]

Perhaps more than any other nation in the world, the United
States is haunted by monetary incentives. While workers naturally want more economic prosperity, so do American businesses.
As a result, firms have gone to great lengths to get their money's worth out of their laborers. To this end, Frederick Winslow
Taylor, an efficiency fixated engineer and America's first management consultant, developed new methods for managers to
extract the maximum productivity out of their charges. As Taylor
devised his methodology, businesses needed to scientifically train
employees, thereby avoiding ineffective production. Supervisors
were also held personally responsible for the efficiency of their
workers, which would potentially lead to strained relationships within that work environment. This would lead critics to
point out that Taylor's demanding supervision lacked any sense
of humanity. Laborers are not mechanical robots. As Henry
Mintzberg pointed out in his 1989 collection on managerial
styles, Taylor's almost maniacal focus on efficiency overshadowed
those less quantifiable social benefits, such as one having pride in
creating a well-crafted product.[55]

While businesses developed advertising schemes to entice
American consumers to buy more and more, they also had to

grapple with making them pay for these goods and services. While most consumers would eventually pay for what they promised to purchase, there were invariably those who either could not—*or would not*—honor their debt obligations.[56]

CHAPTER 11

PAWNSHOPS

A bank is a place that will lend you money
if you can prove you don't need it.

—Comedian Bob Hope

PEOPLE WHO NEEDED CASH quickly and who could not qualify to obtain a loan through a conventional bank had to resort to find other options. Loan sharks have frequently offered fast loans but at exorbitant rates and with severe consequences if one defaulted on repayment. As noted previously, John Mackey, the founder of HFC, was more of a loan shark than a government-sanctioned lender. Another option for the individual in desperate need of cash was to go to a pawnshop.

Upscale pawnshops began to appear in the early twentieth century, often referred to as "loan offices," since the term "pawn shop" had a very negative historical reputation at this point. Some of these so-called loan offices were located on the upper floors of office buildings. The modern euphemism for the upscale pawn shop is the "high-end collateral lender," lending to the upper-class often white-collar individuals, including doctors, lawyers and bankers, as well as more colorful individuals like high-rolling gamblers. They were also interchangeably called "upscale pawnshops" and "high-end pawnshops" due to their acceptance of higher value merchandise in exchange for short-term loans. These objects could include wine collections, jewelry, large diamonds, fine art, cars, and unique memorabilia. Loans were often sought to deal with business revenue shortfalls and other expensive fiscal issues.

Collateral has been a contractual device used by lenders around the world to ensure that their cash advances are protected. The lender can seize these assets if the borrower does not make the agreed-upon payments on the loan, so the lender has some protection if the borrower defaults. Many are familiar with the Shakespearian tale of the *Merchant of Venice*. In the play, a pound of the character Antonio's flesh is collateralized in exchange for Shylock's loan to Bassanio. Even when many Europeans desperately needed funds for an item of value, the antisemitic portrayals of pawnbrokers had a chilling effect on those who might have sought financial assistance.[57]

However, this was a fictionalized account and "pawning" is an example of a common type of loan secured with collateral. The pawning process begins when a customer brings an item into a pawn shop. All sorts of items could be pawned or sold outright by customers, but the most common items are things such as jewelry, electronics, collectibles, musical instruments, tools, and, depending on federal, state, and local laws, firearms, gold, silver, and platinum, which are often purchased, even if they are in the form of broken jewelry of little value. Metal can still be sold in bulk to a bullion dealer or smelter for the value by weight of the component metals. Similarly, jewelry that contains genuine gemstones, even if broken or missing pieces, generally have value. In the United States the amount of time, and rate of interest, is governed by law and by the state commerce department policies. They have the same license as a bank, which is highly regulated.

The pawnbroker assesses an item for its condition and marketability by testing the item and examining it for flaws, scratches or other damage. Another aspect that affects marketability is the supply and demand for the item in the community or region. To assess the value of different items, pawnbrokers use guidebooks ("blue books"), catalogs, Internet search engines, and their own experience. Some pawnbrokers are trained in the identification of gems or employ a specialist to assess jewelry. One of the risks of accepting secondhand goods is that the item may be counterfeit. The customer can either sell the item outright if, as in most cases, the pawnbroker is also a licensed secondhand dealer or offer the item as collateral on a loan. Most pawnshops are willing to negotiate the amount of the loan with the client.

In the pawnbroker's defense, he/she assumes the risk that an item might have been stolen. However, laws in many jurisdictions protect both the community and broker from unknowingly handling stolen goods. These laws often require that the pawnbroker establish positive identification of the seller through photo identification (such as a driver's license or government-issued identity document), as well as a holding period placed on an item purchased by a pawnbroker to allow time for local law enforcement authorities to track stolen items. Also, in some states, pawnshops are required to provide a list of all newly pawned items and any associated serial number to local law enforcement, so that it can be determined if any of the items have been reported stolen. Often, law enforcement personnel will advise those victims of burglary or robbery to visit local pawnshops to see if they have obtained stolen items. Some pawnshops set up their own screening criteria to avoid buying stolen property. There are unscrupulous companies that knowingly engaged in purchasing stolen items and selling them on to an unsuspecting public and these illegal operations are known as "fences."

Collateral, especially within banking, traditionally refers to secured lending (also known as asset-based lending). More complex collateralization arrangements may be used to secure trade transactions (also known as capital market collateralization). The former often presents unilateral obligations secured in the form of property, surety, guarantee, and/or other collateral (originally denoted by the term security), whereas the latter often presents bilateral obligations secured by more-liquid assets (such as cash). Collateralization of assets gives lenders a sufficient level of reassurance against default risk. It also helped some borrowers to obtain loans if they had poor credit histories. In addition, collateralized loans generally have substantially lower interest rate than unsecured loans.

Defaulted pawnshop debts, which the U.S. Internal Revenue Service considers to be non-recourse financial obligations, have one distinct advantage over recourse debt: recourse debt holds the borrower personally liable and allows lenders to collect what is owed for the debt even after they have recouped the collateral. Banks and credit card companies, which are usually the same entities, have the right to garnish one's wages, levy accounts, sell the debt to aggressive collection agencies, which have been restrained from employing predatorial tactics by the Fair Debt Collection Practices Act of (FDCPA) of 1978, and negatively impact a borrower's credit score. On the other hand, a non-recourse loan precludes the lender from pursuing anything other than the collateral provided on the debt.

CHAPTER 12

THE ESTABLISHMENT OF THE FEDERAL RESERVE, THE ECONOMIC IMPACT OF THE FIRST WORLD WAR, AND THE ECONOMIC BOOM OF THE 1920S

The long period of U.S. neutrality made the ultimate conversion of the economy to a wartime basis easier than it otherwise would have been.

—Carlos Lozada,
"The Economics of World War I,"
National Bureau of Economic Research Digest
(January 2005)

THE AMERICAN ECONOMY EXPERIENCED a very brief depression—*only from mid-October to November*—in 1907. Nonetheless, due to the deleterious impact it had, America's financial leaders believed that the federal government had to take a more active role in regulating the economy. Following a great deal of pressure, on December 23, 1913, the Senate passed the Federal Reserve Act, the first central banking system since Andrew Jackson's era. After President Woodrow Wilson signed the act into law, an "inelastic currency," that is, a currency that fluctuates in volume with the demands of business, was infused into the market. Now that a central bank had been created, the federal government would never again have to solicit private bankers, such as J. P. Morgan, to ingratiate itself to obtain sufficient capital to keep the banking system afloat. In addition, "runs on the bank," when depositors would make panic withdrawals, were stemmed, however, never completely eradicated.

In August 1914, war broke out in Europe and for two and a half years the United States remained neutral. However, in April 1917, Congress declared war on Germany and federal spending surged as the U.S. military prepared to go to war in France. The government embarked on such a massive spending spree to provide for military enlistments, ordinance, and troop training, that there was a fifteen-fold acceleration in federal outlays. Beyond this, the United States loaned its allies huge amounts and, as a result, spending quickly outpaced the nation's tax revenues. Consequently, the Treasury Department turned to promoting war bonds, celebrated as "liberty loans," to resupply its coffers. In turn, the Treasury enticed the public to "borrow and buy" the bonds or to finance their purchases through their local banks. To sweeten the deal, "the Fed," the shortened name for the Federal Reserve, lent funds to member banks at low interest rates, provided that the proceeds were used to buy war bonds. These bond drives were highly successful and by the spring of 1918, the federal government had sold roughly ten billion dollars in war bonds and other financial instruments.

Although Americans had engaged in personal lending from the time of its founding, until the need to fund America's entry into World War I, lenders had never been permitted to resell their customers' debts or borrow against them. It was at this point that American capitalism began to allow, indeed encourage, personal debt to be legalized, sellable, and profitable. Venture capitalists could see the tremendous possibilities now possible and began specializing in loaning to consumers. Naturally, as time went on, these firms began to refine their techniques for luring customers in and the 1920s could be as easily categorized as the "Age of Advertising" as it could be called the "Jazz Age."

This is not to say that governmental entities, by and large, did not allow this to happen for self-interest or malicious intentions. In most instances, these changes were perceived as viable options for those hampered by unemployment, wealth inequality, and/ or discrimination. Nevertheless, this new paradigm frequently produced significant and unexpected effects on the economy.[58]

Not long after the hostilities in Europe ended and Woodrow Wilson left office, war-weary Americans overwhelmingly elected pro-business, fiscally conservative Warren G. Harding in 1920. Not only had America paid a gigantic price to transport its military to Europe to make "the world safe for democracy," but the influenza pandemic had occurred, there had been severe labor unrest, and the Red Scare heightened an already tense electorate. Harding's call for a "return to normalcy" justified disengaging from foreign affairs and returning to tending to business as usual in America. One of his priorities was stated in his March 4, 1921, inaugural speech: he stood for ensuring that there were adequate credit facilities. Indeed, Harding's vice-president and successor, Calvin Coolidge, would concur and on January 17, 1925, he told the American Society of Newspaper Editors in Washington, D.C. that, ". . . the chief business of the American people is business. They are profoundly concerned with producing, buying, selling, investing and prospering in the world."[59]

Under Harding's short administration (he died of cardiac arrest on August 2, 1923), the economy shifted from the production of capital goods to consumer merchandise. In addition, the Justice Department and Federal Trade Commission, which had been created to enforce civil antitrust law and protect consumers, no longer impeded Big Business. As one investigator noted, the FTC appeared to be committing *hara-kiri*.[60]

The American economy saw a huge upsurge in growth during the 1920s. There were many reasons why the United States prospered while Europe and so much of the rest of the world languished. For one thing, America did not have to suffer the devastation so many countries experienced because the United States was far removed from the fighting. In addition, America possessed ample natural resources and had abundant cheap labor thanks to all the immigrants still pouring in. Moreover, many U.S. businesses reaped large dividends from loans to European nations. Finally, the Great War, as the first truly global conflict was known, spawned new inventions and innovations, especially within the United States.

In the twenties, debt in the United States was defined via two new modalities: installment credit and legalized personal loans. While installment credit afforded American consumers to possess more, retailers to sell more, and manufacturers to produce more—*all at lower prices*—the proclivity of many not to view this new debt as the same as cash debt—that is, making it appear less than what it was—invariably much of the debt would become uncollectable because consumers borrowed well beyond their financial means. Nevertheless, the rise of so much personal debt had a positive component—it provided the industrial workers, who had produced all the additional goods, the chance to directly benefit from the rise in capitalistic manufacturing.[61]

There had been a major cultural shift that occurred in the second decade of the twentieth century. In the 1860s and 1870s, owning luxury products was perceived by many Americans to be a sign of moral corruption; in fact, critics thought owning such items would make men "effeminate, weak, and dependent." However, by the 1920s, the idea had lost its social stigma and, as social critic Samuel Strauss had noted, luxury was now represented "a source of strength" and something granted to the masses.[62]

As previously noted, installment plans available allowed a consumer to purchase something by paying for it monthly and, in turn, many Americans could get their luxury goods now and worry about paying for it later. Since all sorts of advertising and mass marketing campaigns were beginning to be conducted via roadside billboards (that automobiles would pass by), newspaper ads, and short visual promotions (in "movie houses" prior to feature films being shown), large numbers of consumers, who did not differentiate between "wants" from "needs," kept consuming.[63]

Despite experiencing a short downturn in 1921, the U.S. enjoyed unprecedented economic development for the remainder of the decade. As American buyers continued to buy phonographs, automobiles, and soon home radios (in 1923 only one percent of American households possessed a radio, but by 1931, more than half of all U.S. homes had one) through installment credit. For those who were denied a personal loan by lack of sufficient income, lack of collateral, or overextension of debt from previous borrowing, loan sharks would be the only alternative. In the

1920s, these individuals were usually local opportunists looking to provide short-term loans at highly inflated interest rates. They were fundamentally indistinguishable from what exist today as legally sanctioned "pay day" loan companies.[64]

Other individuals facilitated consumer purchases in the Age of Advertising. Edward Louis Bernays, the nephew of Sigmund Freud, had received his early training working on "psychological warfare" as a member of George Creel's Committee on Public Information (America's propaganda machine during World War I). He has been often referred to as "the father of public relations." One of Bernays's best-known campaigns was a 1929 effort to promote female smoking by branding cigarettes as feminist "Torches of Freedom." Bernays was a shrewd promoter who understood the best method ". . . to transform the profane into an imitation of the sacred." Much like Aaron Eckhart's character, Nick Naylor, in the 2005 film *Thank You for Smoking* film, he was renowned for his ability to entice people into purchasing products that they had never originally wanted. Indeed, in the spring of 1924, Bernays oversaw a "saturation campaign" for "transparent velvet" (a lightweight, sheer fabric also known as chiffon velvet) to stimulate three and half million American women to see it as something they *had to have*. Historian Daniel Borstein's 1962 book, *The Image: A Guide to Pseudo-Events in America*, has credited Bernays as being the originator of "pseudo-events," that is, while employing hype, Bernays arranged events merely for the sake of the publicity they generated, particularly those designed to appear spontaneous or unplanned. For instance, when a mayor "cuts the ribbon" at the grand re-opening of a historic hotel or when the president "pardons a turkey," these are examples of staged affairs choreographed by Bernays. Another favorite ploy of Edward Bernays was to have a celebrity or political figure call a press conference to clarify some misunderstanding or misrepresentation, but the underlying motive was just to divert people's attention to ultimately sell products. These antics have often been referred to as "hyperreality" and in more recent times they have been dubbed "fake news."[65]

In boom times, of course, people still went bankrupt. For example, in 1922 Will Rogers founded his own production company and made three motion pictures in the same year. Unfortunately, Rogers's effort to create his own conduit for financing his motion pictures was a catastrophe. He had mortgaged his home, his life insurance policy, and the Liberty Bonds he had purchased for his children. Indeed, according to Betty Rogers, Will's wife, the couple even had to borrow money from the films themselves. Since the Oklahoma social critic had spent everything he had on the three films, when they all flopped at the box office, he had to close his production company and slowly rebuild his career by booking more performances than he had in the past.[66]

President Calvin Coolidge praised America's national prosperity in an address he gave in 1927. He urged people to keep buying and Will Rogers, already concerned about growing consumer debt, responded: "so that leaves us without any economic problem whatever, except perhaps someday having to pay for them."[67]

Chapter 13

Economic Calamity

*I can assure you that it is safer to keep your money
in a reopened bank than under the mattress.*

—President Franklin Delano Roosevelt
in his first Fireside Chat, March 12, 1933

THE GREAT DEPRESSION, THE longest and most drastic economic downturns in the U.S. experience, began at the end of the 1920s and did not fully recover until shortly after America's entry into World War II. During the twenties, there had been a dramatic upswing in the American economy and stock values rose precipitously. For the first time, Americans of ordinary means used much of their disposable income or even mortgaged their homes to buy stocks. The economy continued to do well, and it seemed to many that there was no reason to believe it would not continue; indeed, as the decade neared the end, investors were gambling that the market would continue to rise by purchasing stock shares "on margin." This meant that their stock purchase was financed with loans to be repaid with profits generated from the seemingly ever-increasing share prices. The standard practice was that the investor would put ten percent down and then finance the remaining ninety percent by using the marginable securities in their brokerage account as collateral.

Once prices began to decline in October 1929, millions of over-extended shareholders fell into panic and rushed to liquidate their holdings, exacerbating the stock market's fall and creating further economic havoc. The U.S. economy went into freefall as manufacturing, banking, and commerce imploded; however, the agricultural sector, which had profited from feeding American troops during World War I, started its long downward cycle well before the industrial or commercial components due its continued overproduction of foodstuffs and its need to purchase modern, mechanized farming equipment.[68]

To respond to people withdrawing their bank deposits, newly elected President Franklin D. Roosevelt called a special session of Congress and declared a four-day banking holiday. FDR closed all banks, including the Federal Reserve. On March 9, 1933, Congress passed the Emergency Banking Act, which helped to partially restore public confidence.

Nevertheless, the economy continued to falter. One of the complicating matters was created by intense dust storms that beset the American plains. In three different waves, 1934, 1936, and 1939-1940, blinding sand columns swept over formerly fertile grain fields of Kansas, Colorado, Oklahoma, Texas, and New Mexico. With falling prices and inadequate yields on their crops, many farmers were forced into foreclosure and abandoned their family farms. On the national level, this led to a paucity of food and with an unemployment rate hovering around twenty-five percent and the emerging danger of malnutrition as well as potential starvation for some families, one of President Roosevelt's New Deal programs, the Federal Emergency Relief Act (FERA), budgeted seventy-five million dollars to provide food for destitute people.

America was still gripped in the Great Depression and this caused some to have to abandon even miniscule savings payments and most lending institutions discarded savings programs altogether. Concurrently, some unethical bankers choose to charge creditworthy customers at usurious rates for personal loans rather than assisting them as loyal savers. To try to halt predatory banking practices, Congress passed the Glass-Steagall Act of 1933, which was part of the Banking Act (amended as part of the 1935 Banking Act), It mandated that investment banking, commercial banking, insurance practices, and residential-mortgage lending were disparate and highly regulated industries. Moreover, Glass-Steagall specifically prohibited retail banks from taking part in any component of investment banking. In 1999, the Glass-Steagall era came to an end when the Gramm-Leach-Bliley Act (GLBA, which is sometimes mockingly referred to as the "Citigroup Funding Act") repealed the Glass-Steagall's restrictions on the relationships between commercial and investment banks (and partially repealed other elements).[69] While Glass-Steagall clearly helped to stave off economic stress for decades, some have contended that its repeal either was a cause of the financial crisis that resulted in the 2008 financial meltdown ". . . or that it fueled and worsened the crisis's deleterious effect."[70]

For hundreds of thousands of Americans, just having nourishment and shelter became the grim reality. A popular song during this era was *Brother, Can You Spare a Dime?* and "Hoovervilles," makeshift encampments erected with cardboard, old lumber, tar paper, or whatever materials could be found, housed the thousands of homeless Americans. These shanty towns were named after Herbert Hoover, the president at the time, whose inability to stem the tide of the economic meltdown perturbed desperate Americans. As they saw it, he was either too timid to take bold action or he was just downright incompetent.[71]

Although the first American commercial bank, that is, a bank created to invest in businesses exclusively, the Bank of North America, was established on January 4, 1782, it was not until the late 1930s that commercial banks ventured into the realm of consumer financing.[72] Mackey and other banks had demonstrated just how lucrative extracting profits from consumer loans could be and, after all, during the Depression, personal debt was now pervasive.

CHAPTER 14

WORLD WAR II AND ITS IMPACT ON THE POSTWAR ECONOMY

I was fascinated by the culture clash between England and America in the 1950s. My first memories are of being a girl in those postwar years when things were really pretty grim. It wasn't like in America, which was [a] real boom time.

—Novelist Laurie Graham

IT IS INTERESTING THAT the same sequence of events pretty much occurred and then was replicated again for the United States during both the global conflicts and the postwar years. Once America was attacked by Imperial Japan in December 1941, the United States declared war. Now America found itself again fighting, but this time across two oceans. Most large corporations shifted their production of consumer goods to manufacturing the instruments of war to support not only American military personnel but also to assist its Allies through the congressionally approved Lend-Lease Act, which had been in place since March 1941. Employment surged and those who had not already volunteered or been drafted into the military worked in agriculture or the war industries.

As the war neared its close in the summer of 1945, America's outlook was disquieting. While the war in Europe had been won, Imperial Japan was determined to kill hundreds of thousands of Americans invaders if they attempted to breech the four Japanese islands. In addition, America's wartime ally, the Soviet Union, was increasingly asserting its right to control the lands it "liberated" from the Third Reich. Due to the ominous threat of Soviet expansion, the business community was uncertain whether it would be able to shed its war production and return to peacetime manufacturing.

Despite the threat from massive losses invading Japan, America ushered in the nuclear age with the atomic destruction of two major Japanese cities and the war in the Pacific ended. Also, even though tensions between the United States and the Soviet Union only intensified into a full-blown Cold War, America's economy, again as it had after World War I, was rejuvenated. While the radio captivated Americans in the 20s and 30s, television would do the same in the 40s and 50s.

Since Americans had endured so long either in uniform overseas or contending with rationing and food deprivation at home, Americans were more than ready to splurge. In addition, the forced frugality had allowed many to tuck away wartime savings. As U.S. industries moved from manufacturing weapons of war to products of leisure and convenience, economic growth surged. With improved cars now on the market making transportation easier, many former urban and rural dwellers moved in massive numbers to the suburbs.

The Cold War was good for business, as defense spending assisted in America's economic growth. Labor unions were able to assert more power at the negotiating tables and workers' wages increased. Even after the three-year Korean War had ended, the good times continued and the United States was labeled as "the affluent society," based on the title of economist John Kenneth Galbraith's 1958 examination of contemporary America. Galbraith argued that the 1950s was aptly named the affluent society due to the era's accelerated production joined with a vast array of consumer goods. Americans saw their paychecks grow while poverty slackened a bit. One must bear in mind that while white males were the primary beneficiaries during this epoch, people of color were still severely hampered by segregation. Also, women were largely relegated to domestic work and the three major work opportunities for them were becoming flight attendants, schoolteachers, or business secretaries.

Chapter 15

Credit Cards and
Consumer Confidence

*Banks introduced the installment plan. The
disappearance of cash and the coming of the credit
card changed the shape of life in the United States.*

—Jerzy Kosinski,
author of *Being There*

CREDIT CARDS, WHICH ARE now as ubiquitous as cell phones, were initiated by Frank X. McNamara, one of the four founders of Diners' Club International, because he was hosting clients at a restaurant in 1949 and discovered that he had inadvertently left his wallet in a different suit. MacNamara asked his wife to pay the bill. Due to this incident, McNamara came up with an idea: why not create a charge card so that something like his *faux pas* would not occur again.

In the beginning, the Diner's Club credit card was free to the customer. Diner's Club made its money from charging a six percent transaction fee to the merchant. This expense would be worth it to many companies if, naturally, it brought in more customers. However, at this time only people of wealth could qualify for the credit card and, as Diner's Club's first director of marketing, stated, "it was a card for people who could afford to carry what amounted to a blank check."[73]

Credit cards became more accessible and imbued into the American economy in the 1970s and 80's due to a series of federal banking-law developments that eased regulations on federally insured depositories, mortgage lenders, credit card lenders, and other financial companies. These changes gave the lending entities broad rights to disregard state usury interest laws.[74]

Today, when one applies for a credit card, or an existing member requests a limit increase, credit analysts, who employ an algorithm, determine which applicant will obtain a card or receive the credit increase. The former director of Capital One's "revolver proactive credit limit increase program," has recounted how the inner workings of the industry's well-oiled debt machine operated. She described it as:

> . . . a system of experimentation, product design, marketing, and underwriting practices engineered to push those Americans who could be pushed into as much debt as they could be pushed into, without, ideally, pushing them over the edge into default.[75]

Americans have been strongly encouraged to go into debt, if only to create a favorable credit history that, in turn, will benefit them if-and-when they need to secure a personal loan.[76] Thanks to more consumers being able to qualify—*even if only marginally*—for credit cards, many have gone into debt to achieve such goal.

Unfortunately, despite their best intentions, large numbers have failed to handle the cards properly and found themselves simply stuck with debt and an unfavorable credit history.

As with virtually everything else in the human world, financial ruin could occur and certainly banks, savings and loans, and credit unions, particularly in early years, have had to assume risk and liability to extend credit to so many consumers. As has been previously documented, lending institutions developed sophisticated and largely reliable methods of scrutinizing prospective borrowers. Furthermore, Americans were admonished to take great care of their borrowing history because if one were to be labeled with the "Q.C." (questionable credit) designation, his/her reputation would be severely tarnished.[77] As a result, *only a little over three percent* of Americans' total outstanding credit card balances are thirty days or more delinquent. While the many of these delinquencies are because "life happens" and, if something akin to an emergency hospitalization occurs to those without sufficient medical insurance, a "rainy day fund" will not come close to covering the exorbitant medical charges that they owe, there will always be those who default despite their best intentions. For example, an older man decided to fulfill his "bucket list" wish of going on a trip around the world. However, due to the rigors of all that travel, he arrives back at his home and dies of a massive heart attack. Who will pay off that huge bill he racked up on his $20,000 credit-limit credit card? His children? No, they are immune to their father's credit card debt[78] and, in turn, the credit card lender must absorb this large loss. Nevertheless, as Carl Webb, a comanager of Ford Financial Fund (a Dallas-based private equity firm that provides equity investments to various financial institutions) observed, "Banks get in trouble for one reason: They make bad loans."[79] Banks are aware of such contingencies, and this is why most card users are "contained" within strict credit limits. Oh, yes, credit reporting firms document all the lines of credit an individual may possess, and lenders generally will not be caught off guard by a person's increased liability.

One other element came into play in the late sixties that made the lending industry squeamish: the advent of gaging consumer confidence within the national economy. In 1967, a non-profit, nonpartisan association of business leaders formed the Consumer Confidence Index (CCI). The group's goal was to determine the faith that consumers had in the overall financial well-being of the American economy. The Conference Board releases a monthly report entitled the "Consumer Confidence Index" (CCI) and it submits both a "Present Situation Index" along with an "Expectations Index." In December 1985, ABC News thought it would be noteworthy to report on the current state confidence that American consumers had in the economy. Known as the "ABC News Consumer Comfort Index," this new polling process had an unforeseen consequence: when lenders could see that consumer confidence was low, to protect their positions, they started to reduce credit card approvals, limit increases on personal accounts, and so forth. Conversely, when consumer confidence was high, the lending institutions gave more card approvals, increased the limits on personal accounts, and so on. Although University of Michigan Professor George Katona developed his own consumer confidence index in the late 1940s, the expanded University of Michigan Consumer Sentiment Index (MCSI) would expand the process to assess more components of the economic mood of the country, such as consumer spending, the latest business adjustments, and trends in individual finances. Today, the MCSI and the Conference Boards Consumer Confidence Index are the most widely followed measures of U.S. consumer confidence. Critics have argued that such indices frequently provide a tilted appraisal of consumer sentiment since some of the indices' questions generate more predictive power than others. On the other hand, those inquiries that ". . . ask about consumers' perceptions of job availability typically have the most explanatory power for future movements in consumption." Furthermore, questions that venture into the current purchasing environment or the financial situation vis-à-vis previous periods seem to possess much less explanatory power.[80]

To alleviate wasting too much of their time and resources, when a credit card holder has not made at least the minimum payment for his/her last billing cycle, credit card agencies will sell the account to a debt collection agency for generally *four percent of the original debt value*. The collection agency will then attempt to collect the full balance of the account. This afforded the debt purchasers a gigantic return if the debtor remitted the amount in full; consequently, debt collectors had been notorious for employing all sorts of deceptive acts or unfair practices to try to extract the balance owed from the delinquent credit card holders.

Until the beginning of the second decade of the twenty-first century, these delinquent card holders were frequently subjected to almost around the clock phone calls at home as well as at their places of employment. The collection agents often used obscene, derogatory, and insulting language and threatened to use violence or other criminal measures to intimidate the indebted person. There were some people who either attempted to kill themselves or succeeded. Due to the widespread abuse of these consumers, the U.S. Congress passed the "Credit Card Accountability Responsibility and Disclosure Act of 2009," which is generally referred to as "the CARD Act."[81] In a nutshell, the CARD Act is an amendment to the Truth in Lending Act of 1968 and it mandates transparent credit card disclosures and requires fair and equitable treatment to the delinquent borrowers. The CARD Act expands on those rights and places limits on issuers' fees, rate increases, and marketing practices. The CARD Act also places strict limits on debt collectors. They are usually forbidden from contacting anyone in the collections process before eight a.m. or after nine p.m. and a debt collector may not harass the person in collections over the phone or through any other form of contact, including text or email. They are prohibited from employing social media to publicly post anything concerning an alleged debt. They are allowed to contact a debtor privately on social media *only if* the borrower has consented to use this contact form. If the debt collector communicates with someone in collections using "an email address, telephone text number, or other electronic medium," they must offer a reasonable and simple method for the person in collections to opt out. Finally, if a debt collector has been notified that an attorney is representing someone in collections, the collector is usually required to contact the attorney representing the person in collections directly. The CARD Act has gone a long way to shore up the badgering, intimidating, and often downright cruel behavior of the more predatorial collection agents.

Shortly after the start of the Covid 19 Pandemic, March 11, 2020, to May 5, 2023, according to the World Health Organization, credit card balances in the United States decreased significantly in the second quarter of 2020. This was the largest quarterly decline on record.[82] Unfortunately, it did not take long after the end of the pandemic that credit card balances skyrocketed to their previous levels.

There is potential for some relief for those contending with excessively high credit card interest rates. A bipartisan bill sponsored by Senators Josh Hawley (R-MO) and Bernie Sanders (I-VT) would place a limit of ten percent rate on all credit cards for one year. Currently, the average credit card rate is over twenty percent, which Hawley characterized as "exploitive."[83]

Finally, while most credit card holders may not even be aware of it, lending institutions are beginning to charge them more in advance every time they use their cards. Merchants pay anywhere from 1.5% to 3.5% for each transaction, but they also often must pay for the right to accept credit and debit cards, or "swipe fees." Retailers have begun to challenge the higher end costs for consumers using a two or three percent cash back card and, at times, they will tack on a surcharge. It is advisable if one is dining out that he/she brings along cash or a debit card if the surcharge is added.[84]

Chapter 16

Payday Loans

*These are loans of desperation and they generate
their own need and ongoing desperation.*

—Ellen Harnick, executive vice president
at the Center for Responsible Lending

Payday loans, often referred to as payday advances, are short-term unsecured cash payments, that is, loans without collateralized assets to assure the lender that something of tangible value can be taken in the event of the borrower defaulting on the debt, are usually limited from three hundred to one thousand dollars. These cash advances generally require repayment within two weeks and certainly by the forthcoming payday. Since most banks ceased making small cash loans to consumers in the late 1990s, payday lenders saw an opportunity to fill this void and to make huge profits through high interest rates, late fees, and sometimes automatic loan renewals that the borrower did not see and/or understand that were included in his/her contract.

Many individuals who seek payday loans are low-income individuals. These borrowers live from paycheck to paycheck and when an unforeseen financial emergency arises, such as a car repair, need to make a car payment, or a medical crisis, these desperate people have no choice but to apply for a payday loan. They are aware of the exorbitant interest rate that will be added to their loan; however, they will often not look carefully at the fine print in the terms and conditions of their loans that require the borrower to notify the lender that they do not want the loan automatically renewed. Even in those cases where the loans are not automatically renewed (or the borrower opts out of the option in advance), the high fee that the borrower had to pay on his/her initial loan put them in a deficient spending spiral that requires them to go back at the end of the next month and repeat the same process. Having to take out second and third loans is known as a "rollover" and this only moves the consumer closer to being in a "debt trap." This is a situation in which a financial obligation is virtually impossible to be repaid by the debtor, invariably due to high interest payments precluding the borrower from repaying the principal. Naturally, the interest has not been remitted either and that portion is then wrapped into the aggregate. Concurrently, of course, the payday loan companies prosper.

Many states prohibit usurious loans, that is, excessive interest rates applied to loan repayment. Also, the "Truth in Lending Act of 1968" (TILA) requires lenders to disclose loan stipulations to a borrower before extending credit. The most important of these requirements are that the annual percentage rate (APR), the term of the loan, and the total costs to the borrower be provided in advance. In addition, some states limit the APR that any lender, including payday lenders, can charge and, as of this examination (April 2025), twelve states prohibit payday lending. Also, the rates of these loans were formerly restricted in most states by the "Uniform Small Loan Law" (USLL).[85] Two-thirds of the states have adopted some form of the law.

It is true that the payday loan companies are taking risks in lending to individuals who have either poor credit ratings or are too new to the job market to have secured a profile rating. Also, since these loans are unsecured, they must rely on obtaining account information and employing collection agencies to ensure that the loans are repaid. However, just as in the case of any other lending institution, measures are in place to ensure that the payday loan company does not lose. Naturally, casinos and other gambling establishments operate in the same way.

Consumers need to always be alert because unscrupulous and predatory cash advance firms, accompanied by usurers, loan sharks, and other unscrupulous lenders, often operate outside banking restrictions. Despite being a violation of the law, these scoundrels have been known to drain the borrower's bank account(s) when the trusting consumers surrender their account's information.

CHAPTER 17

THE BANKRUPTCY REFORM ACT OF 1978

High bankruptcy rates, increased credit card debt, and identity theft make it imperative that all of us take an active role in providing financial and economic education at all stages of life.

—Ruben Hinojosa (D-TX),
former U.S. Representative
who served on the Subcommittee
on FinancialInstitutions and Consumer Credit

IN 1978, THE U.S. Congress enhanced and augmented the authority of the federal bankruptcy courts. Judges were given greater discretion regarding which businesses would be liquidated (Chapter 7) or allowed to continue to operate with a court-appointed trustee (Chapter 11). The goal of the Chapter 11 provision was that the firm could then reorganize and, in time, rehabilitate itself into a viable enterprise once again. To oversee the rehabilitation, the bankruptcy court will assign a Chapter 11 trustee with "the absolute priority rule," which means the trustee has the authority to decide the portion of the bankruptcy applicant's remaining assets that will be made to each participant. In all cases, secured claims are given preference over unsecured claims. In turn, debts owed to creditors will be paid off first and then shareholders divide the remaining assets.

In some cases, individuals may file for bankruptcy under the auspices of Chapter 11, and this option is increasingly popular because it provides instant relief because creditors are temporarily prohibited from taking any action against the individual. Both businesses and individuals that are allowed to file under Chapter 11 have four months in which to provide the court with a reorganization plan, although that can be extended to eighteen months.

Regarding Chapter 7, "the absolute priority rule" also applies to individuals who are liquidating their assets to settle claims. For those people who are facing unmanageable bills, the court may allow for a Chapter 13 filing. This provision was generated to save individuals from losing their homes via foreclosure and allowing them to consolidate their debts into a single payment plan. Since there are normally court fees required to file for bankruptcy, a Chapter 13 filing allows the individual to pay their fees over the life of the repayment structure; hence, up-front costs can be eliminated.[86] While they occur in only very rare instances, a bankruptcy court has the discretion to waive fees completely.

CHAPTER 18

THE INCEPTION OF THE FICO SCORING SYSTEM

*Isn't it sad that we have to gain control of the
artificial numbers placed upon us by others
to regain some control of our lives?*

—Rick Gregory, Credit, Privacy,
and Reputation Senior Consumer Analyst

A LTHOUGH VARIOUS METHODS OF estimating
creditworthiness existed before, modern credit scoring models dated to 1989, when Bill Fair and Earl Isaac created Credit
Application Scoring Algorithms, their first credit scoring system,
were introduced. Since the 1990s, when one's creditworthiness
has been vetted by a lending institution, it has been invariably
measured by Fair Issac's three-digit FICO score. The far-reach-
ing effect of this rating system is profound. Even some *employ-
ers, health care providers, home and apartment rental agencies,* and
utility companies, will reference FICO scores; consequently, a low
FICO score could potentially cause one to lose a job, be denied
health insurance, a rental property, or obtain electricity, water,
gas, and trash removal.[87]

As we have previously seen, prior to the advent of creditors employing a credit scoring system, credit was determined by established lending institutions based on credit reports obtained from various credit-reporting bureaus. During the late 1950s, banks started using computerized credit scoring to evaluate one's creditworthiness based abstract statistical risk. When the Equal Credit Opportunity Act banned denying credit on gender or marital status in 1974, along with race, nationality, religion, age, or receipt of public assistance in 1976, banks developed credit scoring systems to protect themselves from potential discrimination lawsuits. Today's "Big Three" consumer credit rating businesses are Equifax, Experian, and TransUnion.

During the 1970s and 80s, the credit reporting industry established increasingly refined prescreening techniques. However, it was not until the Federal Home Loan Mortgage Corporation (FHLMC), now known as "Freddie Mac," began to employ the FICO score in 1995 that it was ushered into the public consciousness.[88]

CHAPTER 19

THE INDENTURED GENERATION

Bankruptcy laws allow companies to smoothly reorganize, but not college graduates burdened by student loans.

—Robert Reich,
former Secretary of Labor

O N JUNE 30, 2023, the U.S. Supreme Court struck down the Biden administration's order to cancel approximately $400 billion in student loans in a 6-3 vote. The justices ruled that the Biden administration overstepped its authority by writing off these loans in the previous year. The administration stated that approximately forty-three million Americans would have benefitted from the loan forgiveness program and that around half of those borrowers would have had the entirety of their student loans forgiven.[89]

The Supreme Court decision was widely celebrated by many Americans. They had been outraged by the Biden administration's attempt to transfer hundreds of billions of dollars in student loan debt on to the backs of taxpayers. After all, why should skilled trades people, business owners, or many of the low-income laborers without college degrees who had worked hard to achieve their livelihoods developed their skills and businesses and who had been responsible borrowers, now be burdened with the debt left behind by these frequently imprudent young people? America has always stood for fairness, and this is truly the opposite of fairness.

In addition, critics pointed to the fact that the real culprit in all this is the exorbitant rise in the cost of an undergraduate education. The average cost of college, including tuition and ancillary fees, at public four-year institutions has gone up 141.0% over the last two decades and the average annual increase is roughly seven percent.[90] Part of the problem is that many states have shifted the cost of university education to the student. Nevertheless, the reality is that the United States needs to find a solution to the high costs of college. Ultimately, this is at least a big part of the reason that most students must take out loans. Consequently, a temporary solution via a bailout will not remedy the problem for future students who will still have to take large loans to get their education. Of course, the burden could be alleviated if students went to low-cost community colleges, many who are renowned for their academic rigor, for their lower-division coursework and then they would only have to fund their upper-division education.

So, what is the argument for cancelling the current student loan debt? First, the relief that is provided for most debts under the United States Bankruptcy Code is not available for student loan debt and because of this, education debt servitude, aptly referred to as "student indentured servitude," will last a lifetime for tens of thousands of the current generation. Indeed, federal lawmakers have lumped such debt ". . . together with offenses such as fraud, willful injury, and failure to pay child support."[91] Simultaneously, medical bills, *credit card debt, auto loans,* and *even gambling debt* can be canceled by declaring bankruptcy but discharging student loan debt is virtually impossible. Second, the CARD Act has had a deleterious impact on the student indentured generation because its passage has made it very difficult for these new members of the workforce to obtain a credit card since their high debt-to-income ratio disqualified them.[92]

It would be in the best interest of the nation's economic welfare if the Bankruptcy Code should be amended to allow a student loan to be revalued to its actual fair market value. Matters are only going to get worse since the problems of education debt are likely to grow more acute due to lower government funding for education and stagnating income in a tough economy, particularly amid the tariff war that has been inaugurated by the Trump administration. A recent report concludes that rising levels of student debt cause many Americans to delay events such as buying a car, purchasing a home, getting married, and even having children. As one borrower laments, "[h]ow could I consider having children if I can barely support myself?" Some people even avoid dating other people whose student debt level seems excessive.[93] Finally, one must look at just how lucrative funding student loans has been for the private sector. The student loan industry is a massive, profit-making enterprise with loan assets of one trillion dollars, and lending in 2013 exceeding $150 billion; consequently, the student loan business eclipses almost any private industry in annual sales.[94]

CHAPTER 20

INDEBTEDNESS: ONE OF AMERICA'S UNIQUE QUALITIES

Neither a borrower nor a lender be.

–Polonius's advice to his son,
Laertes, Act 1, Scene 3, *Hamlet*

A S EARLY ENGLISH COLONISTS prepared to depart for the New World, their leader, John Winthrop, believed that they were going to create something truly unique and wonderful in their new homeland. On March 21, 1630, Winthrop, the soon-to-be governor of the first Puritan colony, delivered a lecture highly infused with religious rhetoric to his congregation under the title, "A Model of Christian Charity." In his discourse, Winthrop injected his belief that he and his flock were about to embark upon a mission to make their new community in a strange new land the same as righteous Christians individually do. In this manner, Winthrop stated, their "Citty Upon a Hill" will become a "beacon of hope" for the rest of the world. Later, English colonists and then American Patriots, and, even after that, U.S. presidents, would invoke this concept of *"American exceptionalism."* Consequently, even before America was a nation, its English developers thought their new enclave would be "distinctive, unique, and exemplary."[95]

It is important to note that while Winthrop's religious credentials were undeniably authentic, it is also equally important to
point out that his family had been one of the beneficiaries of
Henry VIII's dissolution of the monasteries between 1536 and
1541. The Winthrop family received a five-hundred-acre estate,
which they named Groton Manor, and it greatly enriched them.
Nevertheless, a dramatic downturn in farm prices and rents in
1630 seriously jeopardized the prosperity of the Winthrop household. In consequence, Winthrop's decision to lead his Puritan
flock to the New World in 1630 may have been motivated more
by economic hardship than his religious conviction.[96]

Furthermore, following the War of Independence and the estab-
lishment of the United States, the founders of the new nation
fashioned an entirely new form of government. Instead of power
emanating from a divine-right monarch, powerful prince, or
"Oriental potentate," in the American experiment, all power is
derived from the bottom up—that is, from the people to those
individuals chosen to oversee and administer the government.
This was something truly extraordinary when one considers what
the world had experienced up to the last third of the eighteenth
century. The new government also provided a remedy for those
leaders who would abuse the power given to them by the people.
As the Preamble of the Declaration of Independence stated and
the U.S. Constitution affirmed, those individuals who ruled in an
arbitrary, self-serving, and corrupt manner, would then be subject
to impeachment and removal. This innovation alone is perhaps
the most "revolutionary" of all the founders' reforms; however,
regrettably, this component has always been predicated on an
ideal—the belief that principled leaders would always serve the
interests of the people first.

Naturally, "American exceptionalism" and governmental power emanating from the people heralded virtuous characteristics. Unfortunately, the United States currently holds the distinction of incarcerating more people—over 1.8 million—than any other nation in the world. Communist China, an autocratic nation with a one and a reputation for imprisoning dissents, ranks second with an estimated prison population of 1.69 million people, but it has a population *four times greater* than America.[97]

Just as leading the world in imprisoning people has never been seen as a noble attribute, America has also been a country plagued with debt, both at the national level as well as the personal, since its formation. As previously noted, as of March 2025, America possesses the world's biggest national debt, and it is steadily growing every year.

Granted, many of America's earliest European inhabitants had no choice but to go into debt if they wanted to escape the oppressive class system of their native lands. Beyond this, those who were able to complete their indentured servitude to attain their freedom were often unskilled and impoverished. Time and again, these indigent lower-class workers had to struggle just to accrue sufficient wages to survive and for many that meant having to go into debt again.

In terms of individual household debt, America currently ranks eighteenth in the world. While this may sound as if Americans are largely holding their own, remember that millions of Americans find themselves deeply in debt due to the high balances that they have been retaining on their credit cards. Nationally, credit card debt is approaching $1.7 trillion and the average individual credit card balances at the end of 2024 hit their highest levels in twelve years.

There are so many elements that keep so many Americans in debt. Obviously, the national government sets a poor example, but it has the luxury of extending the debt ceiling and printing more money. Individuals do not have that option.

One factor is that lures people into debt is the "buy now, pay later" enticement sellers employ. One of the most insidious ploys that advertisers use is the "no money down and 24-months to pay" option. Such an inducement will frequently go automatically to a penalty rate of upwards to *thirty percent* if the account is not paid in full within the promotional period. Moreover, the penalty rate is not only applied to the remaining balance, but to the original total purchase as well. Indeed, the promoters will compute the monthly payment into this ostensibly great deal just to attract the prospective buyer into the so-called deal. Finally, other traps are also generated, such as randomly halting monthly payments and then the purchaser is made responsible for the late fees as well as the tacked-on penalty. The online Synchrony Bank, formerly G.E. Capital Retail Bank, has been fined for these sorts of activities.[98]

As we have previously seen, numerous prominent American writers fostered movements that encouraged Americans to go into debt. William James's "New Thought" advocacy and the 'mind-cure' movement invoked the idea of "live and let live," which seemed innocuous enough, but the financial element encouraged people to enjoy life to the fullest, which meant buying things on credit with the anticipation it will simply be paid off later. One of the movement's most influential devotees, L. Frank Baum, the author of *The Wonderful Wizard of Oz*, it will be recalled, supported these "live it up" viewpoints and had to continue churning out more stories of the *Oz* series just to keep himself financially afloat. In the 1920s, "the Age of Advertising," Paul Mazur, a senior partner of Lehman Brothers, wrote that, "We must shift America from a *needs*—to a *desires*—culture. People must be trained to desire, to want new things, even before the old have been entirely consumed. . . . Man's *desires* must overshadow his *needs*."[99] Edward Bernays, the father of public relations, resorted to "hyperreality" schemes to entice people to purchase products they did not want. Of course, this sentiment is still pervasive in the United States.

Another issue that forces consumers to want more, even if they have overextended their capacity to pay, is that some firms have resorted to designing and manufacturing gadgets that are purposefully intended to break down. Termed "planned obsolescence," it was first ascribed to Alfred P. Sloan, Jr., the CEO of General Motors, who in 1924 encouraged his managers to create new car models annually just to keep sales moving upward. In other instances, some manufacturers designed products that would deteriorate quickly or simply become obsolete, thereby forcing buyers to get the more efficient or latest model.

In the modern garment industry, American consumers have the luxury of purchasing "fast fashion," which pertains to all the clothing brands that manufacture massive volumes and do so at minimal cost. This gives the fashion-conscious buyer the opportunity to get the latest trends in clothing rapidly and cheaply. However, such an abundance of inexpensively made clothes has convinced many of those already in debt with the illusion that these new items are *not that much*. Aside from leading to the huge growth of textile waste, pollution, and the depletion of natural resources, fast fashion deludes western buyers that it does not matter how little the item costs, no one is harmed for looking good when the reality is that destitute people living in third world nations make a pittance for these disposable garments.

One other component is unique to the United States. This is the feeling among many consumers that one must financially compete with fellow Americans to live well. The idea originated with Arthur R. "Pop" Momand's cartoon strip, *Keeping up with the Joneses*, in 1913. The parody was featured in the *New York World* newspaper and later syndicated so it could appear in many other papers in America. The comic strip portrayed the status seeking McGinis family, who must struggle to "keep up" with their neighbors, the Joneses. Part of the interest in the storyline was that the Joneses never appeared throughout the cartoon strip's run—that they were often spoken of but never shown. Obviously, the saying "keeping up with the Joneses" remained popular long after the comic strip's end.[100] The expression strikes a chord with many people in the U.S. because it highlights the fact that social status once depended on one's family name; however, social mobility in the United States and the rise of consumerism change this paradigm. With the increasing availability of goods, people became more inclined to define themselves by what they possessed and the quest for higher status accelerated. As we have seen, Thorstein Veblen's 1899 work, *The Theory of the Leisure Class*, addressed this new dynamic by examining conspicuous consumption—the proclivity of so many American consumers to frivolously wield their money to acquire luxury goods and services was misguided at best and downright destructive at worst—and pecuniary emulsion, the tendency of individuals, especially lower wage earners, to desire to emulate the consumption patterns of those with higher status or wealth. As Will Rogers noted, "too many people spend money they haven't earned to buy things they don't want to impress people they don't like."[101]

There are those who have been overwhelmed by catastrophic medical emergencies and in some cases, the rehabilitation costs accompanying the unforeseen issue. In many advanced countries, such emergencies are not a concern because these nations have universal health care. To pay for this luxury, of course, taxes in those countries are exceedingly high; consequently, many Americans are opposed to paying that amount.

PART III: REMEDIES FOR AMERICAN INDEBTEDNESS

CHAPTER 21:

SOLUTIONS

*Debt is like any other trap, easy enough to
get into, but hard enough to get out of.*

—"Josh Billings" (Henry Wheeler Shaw),
nineteenth-century American humorist

S O, WHAT ARE THE solutions? First and most obvious,
do not go into debt. This is naturally more easily said than
done, but as Josh Billings has observed, getting out of debt is
a difficult task. Second, to prepare for life's economic pitfalls,
create an emergency fund that will cover *three to eight* months
of expenses.[102] This will take some time and obviously require
sacrifice, but in most cases, it will provide the necessary money
for when shortfalls arise. Even though one will earn a miniscule amount of interest on most savings accounts in our age, the
emergency money must be kept in a liquid account, so that it is
easily accessible if a critical need arises.

Third, remember that "the frugal live well below their means" and
"being frugal is the cornerstone to wealth-building."[103] Warren
Buffett, the CEO of Berkshire Hathaway and one of the world's
premier investors, has declared that "borrowing money is a fool's
game." Consequently, he has repeated what he had learned when

he studied under investor Benjamin Graham at the Wharton School of the University of Pennsylvania: "rule number one, don't lose money, rule number two, don't forget rule number one, and rule number three, don't go into debt."[104]

Lastly, while you are avoiding the debt trap, develop an investment plan early to provide for your retirement. Personal finance author and radio host, Dave Ramsey, recommends that fifteen percent of an individual's monthly income be placed in "good growth-stock mutual funds."[105]

At the national level, the American executive and legislative branches must begin to collaborate on a federal budget that will address the growing deficit, which is approaching instantiable levels. A debt figure of thirty-six *trillion* dollars is patently absurd.

ENDNOTES

1 Zach Myers, "More Americans under Credit Card Stress," FOX59 News—*Nexstar Media Inc.*, (February 3, 2025), *https://fox59.com/news/more-americans-under-under-credit-card-stress/* (accessed 03-21-2025).

2 "Countries with the Highest National Debt 2025," *World Population Review*, *https://worldpopulationreview.com/country-rankings/countries-by-national-debt* (accessed 03-21-2025).

3 3"Current Federal Debt and Deficit," *Peter G. Peterson Foundation https://www.pgpf.org/programs-and-projects/fiscal-policy/current-debt-deficit/* (accessed 03-21-2025).

4 David Walter Galenson, "The Rise and Fall of Indentured Servitude in the Americas: An Economic Analysis," *The Journal of European History*, Volume 44, Issue 1 (March 1984), p. 1.

5 Jill Lepore, *These Truths: A History of the United States* (New York: W. W. Norton, 2018), p. 226.

6 Axel Madsen, *John Jacob Astor: America's First Multimillionaire*. New York: Wiley & Sons, 2001), p. 12.

7 Denise Kiernan and Joseph D'Agnese, *Signing Their Lives Away: The Fame and Misfortune of the Men who Signed the Declaration of Independence* (Philadelphia: Quirk Books, 2019), p. 272.

8 Lepore, *These Truths*, p. 226.

9 Harold F. See, "Bankruptcy," *The Encyclopedia of the United States Congress* (New York: Simon & Schuster, 995), Volume I, p. 145.

10 See the *Proclamation of the 1825 Treaty of Doak Stand between the United States of America and the Choctaw* (7 Stat., 234), promulgated on February 19, 1825.

11 Joseph J. Ellis, *American Sphinx: The Character of Thomas Jefferson* (New York: Knopf, 1997), p. 287.

12 Tim McGrath, *James Monroe: A Life* (New York: Dutton, 2020), p. 561 and Henry Ammon, *James Monroe: The Quest for National Identity* (New York: McGraw-Hill, 1971), pp. 556–557.

13 See Michael Gerhardt, *Lincoln's Mentors: The Education of a Leader* (New York: HarperCollins, 2021), p. 39; Thomas Keneally, *Abraham Lincoln: A Life* (New York: Penguin, 2008), p. 3; and Jon Meacham, *And There Was Light: Abraham Lincoln and the American Struggle* (New York: Random House, 2022), p. 38.

14 Charles W. Calhoun, *The Presidency of Ulysses S. Grant* (Lawrence: University of Kansas Press, 2017), pp. 583-584.

15 David McCullough, *Truman* (New York: Touchstone, 1992), pp. 149-151 and Robert H. Ferrell, *Harry S. Truman: A Life* (Columbia: University of Missouri Press, 1994), p. 79.

16 McCullough, *Truman*, p. 578.

17 Nancy Isenberg, *Fallen Founder: The Life of Aaron Burr* (New York: Viking, 2007), p. 403.

18 Kiernan and D'Agnese, *Signing Their Lives Away*, p. 41.

19 Doris Kearns Goodwin, *Lyndon Johnson and the American Dream* (New York: St. Martin's Griffin, 1991), p. 24 and p. 82.

20 Josh Lauer, *Creditworthy: A History of Consumer Surveillance and Financial Identity in America* (New York: Columbia University Press, 2017), p. 29.

21 Michael Wallis, *David Crockett: "Lion of the West"* (New York: W. W. Norton, 2011), p. 12.

22 Milton Meltzer, *Edgar Allan Poe: A Biography* (Brookfield, CT: Twenty-First Century Books, 2003), p.123.

23 Lauer, *Creditworthy*, p. 30.

24 Ronald Takaki, *A Different Mirror: A History of Multicultural America* (New York: Back Bay, 2008), p. 155.

25 Ibid., p. 209.

26 Lauer, *Creditworthy*, pp. 27-28.

27 Ibid., pp. 26-27.

28 Olivier Zunz, *The Man Who Understood Democracy: The Life of Alexis de Tocqueville* (Princeton: Princetown University Press, 2022), p. 124.

29 Alexis de Tocqueville, *Democracy in America*, Translated by Arthur Goldhammer (New York: Library of America, 2004), Volume Two, Part III, Chapter 18, pp. 731-732.

30 John Richard Stephens, *Gold: Firsthand Accounts from the Rush that Made the West* (Guilford, CT: Twodot, 2014), p. 10.

31 Richard White, *The Republic for Which It Stands: The United States during Reconstruction and the Gilded Age, 1865-1896* (New York: Oxford University Press, 2017), p. 158.

32 Elena Bottela, *Delinquent: Inside America's Debt Machine* (Oakland: University of California Press, 2022), p. 7.

33 Gilding is a process that involves applying a thin layer of gold to a surface, and this technique was used in the *Gilded* Age to decorate frames, objects, and paintings. The goal was to make objects appear to be gold; however, upon closer inspection, one would be able to see that these items were merely covered with the golden façade. Mark Twain and Charles Dudley Warner coined the term in their 1873 novel *Gilded Age: A Tale of Today*. It was employed as a satire of what some writers had claimed was a "Golden Age."

34 See, "Bankruptcy," Volume I, p. 146.

35 Ana Hernández and Lowell R. Ricketts, "The State of U.S. Wealth Inequality" Federal Reserve Bank of St. Louis (October 22, 2024), *https://www.stlouisfed.org/community-development-research/the-state-of-us-wealth-inequality* (accessed 24-02-2025).

36 Ron Chernow, *Mark Twain* (New York: Penguin, 2025), p. 429-430, p. 433, p. 440, p. 464, p. 475, p. 480, and p. 485.

37 Louis Hyman, *Debtor Nation: A History of America in Red Ink* (Princeton: Princeton University Press, 2011), pp. 11-13. HFC was purchased on March 28, 2003, by the Chinese conglomerate, "The Hongkong and Shanghai Banking Corporation, Limited" (HSBC).

38 Ibid., p. 14.

39 Ibid., p. 15.

40 Science journalist Seth Shulman has written a convincing rebuttal to Bell's claim of having invented the telephone. After meticulously combing through primary documentation as well as reexamining all the inconsistencies in Bell's claims, Shulman concluded that Alexander Graham Bell stole not only Elisha Gray's design for the requisite liquid transmitter to make his device function, but that he was able to solve his problem of getting ". . . varying resistance as a means to convert sound into an electrical signal" only after he had been able to look over the Oberlin College professor's patent application. Although one cannot fully quantify human behavior, Shulman cited numerous instances that he has contended demonstrated Bell's guilt and remorse for attaining all the accolades and wealth that should have been bequeathed to Elisha Gray (as well as Italian inventor Antonio Meucci). Seth Shulman, *The Telephone Gambit: Chasing Alexander Graham Bell's Secret* (New York: W. W. Norton, 2008), pp. 34-38. p. 120, p. 201, and pp. 204-207.

41 Gene Quinn & Steve Brachmann, "Mark Twain: Celebrated American Novelist, Inventor and Champion of a Strong Patent System," *IPA Watchdog* (December 16. 2016), *https://ipwatchdog.com/2016/12/18/mark-twain-novelist-inventor-champion-patent-system/id=75688/* (accessed 27-02-2025).

42 William Leach, *Land of Desire: Merchants, Power, and the Rise of a New American Culture* (New York: Pantheon Books, 1993), p. xiii.

43 Ibid., p. 22.

44 Ibid., p. 28.

45 All the new enticements that department stores used to bring customers in are found in ibid., p. 50, 73, p. 76, and p. 78.

46 See Lauer, *Creditworthy*, p. 6 and p. 18.

47 Ibid., p. 9.

48 Leach, *Land of Desire*, pp. 228-230.

49 Ibid., pp. 232-233.

50 Ibid., p. 245.

51 Ibid., pp. 233-235.

52 Ibid., p. 243.

53 Ibid., p. 246.

54 Ibid., pp. 246-247.

55 Cf. Henry Mintzberg (ed.), *Mintzberg on Management* (New York: The Free Press 1989), p.333 and Lauer, *Creditworthy*, p. 11.

56 Lauer, *Creditworthy*, p. 12.

57 Jewish moneylenders who charged outrageously high interest, such as William Shakespeare's Shylock in the *Merchant of Venice*, Jewish scoundrels and swindlers, like Charles Dickens's Fagin in *Oliver Twist*, underworld gangsters and price fixers, as with F. Scott Fitzgerald's Meyer Wolfsheim in the *Great Gatsby*, and blood-sport boxers as portrayed by Ernest Hemingway's Robert Cohn in The *Sun Also Rises*, are all sinister characters rolled out to depict just how evil Jews are. Jews were envied for their economic success. Finally, the charge of deicide—*that the Jews killed God*—has been used over and over; however, somehow the Romans, who were responsible for imposing the horrific death penalty on Jesus, always avoid blame. Also, Jesus was a Jew, and it has frequently been noted that Jesus was never a true "Christian"—that term was applied to his followers after

his death and supposed resurrection. Mike Rothschild, *Jewish Space Lasers: The Rothschilds and 200 Years of Conspiracy Theories* (Brooklyn: Melville House, 2023), p. 10.

[58] The entire section pertaining to the advent of the Federal Reserve system is extracted from Hyman, *Debtor Nation*, pp. 1-2.

[59] "When a Quote is Not (Exactly) a Quote: The Business of America is Business," *Edition Library of Congress* Blogs: INSIDE ADAMS Science, Technology, and Business (ISSN 2691-3690), https://blogs.loc.gov/inside_adams/2019/01/when-a-quote-is-not-exactly-a-quote-the-business-of-america -is-business-edition/ (accessed 05-03-2025).

[60] In fairness to Harding, as Wilson's second term was coming to its close, the FTC concluded a major investigation into the meatpacking industry and conservative legislators were incensed that the federal agency had the audacity to recommend that the attorney general file a criminal suit against it and, moreover, to recommend that some businesses be nationalized. Senator James Watson (R-IN) accused the FTC of promoting criminal anarchy and sedition. *The New York Times* portrayed the FTC as fomenting "propaganda of a class struggle," and the urged Congress to cure the regulatory agency of its "Bolshevist and propagandist tendencies." Chris Jay Hoofnagle, "The FTC's Historical–and Enduring–Challenges," *Chris Hoofnagle: UC Berkeley School of Law, http://www.law360.com/privacy/articles/753384/ftc-s-early-consumer-protection-challenges-endure* (accessed 10-03-2025).

[61] Hyman, *Debtor Nation*, p. 10. The prosperity of the 1920s also benefited from the electrification of America. As the twenties came to an end, roughly seventy percent of American homes were wired for electricity. Because consumers felt that they had to have the new electric labor-saving devices (irons, fans, vacuum cleaners, toasters, stoves, washing machines, sewing machines, and refrigerators), installment plans were extended to most applicants, which relegated those consumers ". . . at any given moment $2 billion to $3 billions in debt" (and this is when a dollar could buy so much more: today that same dollar would have an equivalent amount in purchasing power of approximately $15.88). Pauline Maier, Merritt Roe Smith, Alexander Keyssar, and Daniel Kevles, *Inventing America* (New York: W. W. Norton, 2003), p. 735.

[62] Leach, *Land of Desire*, pp. 294-295.

[63] Humorist Will Rogers commented, "We are living in an age of publicity. It used to be only saloons and circuses that wanted their name in the paper, but now it's corporations, churches, preachers, scientists, college, and cemeteries." Quoted in Steven Watts, *Citizen Cowboy: Will Rogers and the American People* (New York: Cambridge University Press, 2024), p. 127.

[64] Hyman, *Debtor Nation*, pp. 11-12.

[65] Leach, *Land of Desire*, pp. 319-321.

[66] Watts, *Citizen Cowboy*, p. 118.

[67] Quoted in ibid., p. 150.

[68] Will Rogers summed up the problem by noting that farmers had to figure out "some way to pay back, not some way to borrow more." Ibid., p. 155.

[69] For a more detailed examination of Glass-Steagall and its repeal, see David H. Carpenter, Edward V. Murphy, and Maureen M. Murphy, "The Glass-Steagall

Act: A Legal and Policy Analysis, *Congress.gov* (January 19, 2016) *https://www.congress.gov/crs-product/R44349* (accessed 14-10-2025).

[70] Ibid.

[71] Ibid., p. 296.

[72] John M. Chapman and associates, "Commercial Bank and Consumer Instalment [sic] Credit" in *The Rise of Consumer Financing by Commercial Banks* (Ann Arbor, MI: National Bureau of Economic Research, 1940), p. 12.

[73] Bottela, *Delinquent*, p. 40.

[74] Ibid., p. 12.

[75] Ibid., pp. x-xi.

[76] Hyman, *Debtor Nation*, p. 281.

[77] Lauer, *Creditworthy*, p. 13.

[78] See William Bonner and Addison Wiggen, *Empire of Debt: The Rise of an Epic Financial Crisis* (John Wiley & Sons, 2006), p. 227.

[79] Quoted in Seth Lubove, "After 37 Years, Billionaire Ford Still Eager to Flip Banks for Profit," *The Standard Times: South Coast Today* (August 19, 2012) *https://www.southcoasttoday.com/story/business/2012/08/19/after-37-years-billionaire-ford/49460472007/* (accessed 22-04-2025).

[80] See Jason Bram and Sydney Ludvigson, "Does Consumer Confidence Forecast Household Expenditure? A Sentiment Index Horse Race," *Federal Reserve Bank of New York https://www.google.com/search?q=criticisms+of+consumer+confi-dence+indices&rlz=1C1GCEA_enUS1133US1133&oq=criticisms+of+consumer+-confidence+indces+&gs_lcrp=EgZjaHJvbWUqBggBECEYCjIGCAAQRRg5MgY-IARAhGAoyBwgCECEYjwIyBwgDECEYjwLSAQkzMTMzN2owajSoAgCwAgE&-sourceid=chrome&ie=UTF-8* (accessed 12-04-2025).

[81] See Beverly Harzog, *Confessions of a Credit Junkie: Everything You Need to Know to Avoid the Mistakes I Made* (Pompton Plains, NJ: Career Press, 2014), pp. 56-60.

[82] "COVID-19: Household Debt During the Pandemic," *Congress.gov*, https://www.congress.gov/crsproduct/R46578#:~:text=Mortgage%20debt%20increased%2C%20and%20other,the%202007%2D2009%20Great%20Recession (accessed 05-04-25).

[83] "Credit Cards: A Push to Cap Interest at 10 Percent," *The Week: The Best of the U.S. and International Media* (February 21, 2025), p. 33.

[84] Kelly Dilworth, "Your Money: The Rising Costs of Using a Credit Card," *AARP Bulletin* (January-February 2025), pp. 20-21.

[85] Alex Horowitz, "Economic Mobility and Family Finances," *Consumer Finance* (June 2, 2023), cited in *https://www.pewtrusts.org/en/research-and-analysis/articles/2023/06/02/payday-loans-and-overdraft-a-short-history-and-whats* next#:~:-text=Modern%20payday%20loans%20emerged%20in,in%20more%20than%20 30%20states (accessed 16-02-25) and Bruce G. Caruthers, Timothy W. Guinnane, and Yoonseok Lee, "The Passage of the Uniform Small Loan Law," *Internet Archive* (January 2007), https://web.archive.org/web/20150923203136/http://www.cgdev.org/doc/blog/Roodman%20open%20book/Carruthers,%20Guinnane,%20 and%20Lee,%20The%20Passage%20of%20the%20Uniform%20Small%20 Loan%20Law.pdf. (accessed 16-02-25).

[86] See, "Bankruptcy," I, pp. 145-146.

87 Lauer, *Creditworthy*, p. 15.

88 Ibid.

89 Amy Howe," Supreme Court Strikes Down Biden Student-Loan Forgiveness Program," *SCOTUS Blog Independent News and Analysis of the U.S. Supreme Court*, (June 30, 2023) *https://www.scotusblog.com/2023/06/supreme-court-strikes-down-biden-student-loan-forgiveness-program/* (accessed 08-05-2025).

90 Melanie Hanson, "Average Cost of College by Year," *The Education Data Initiative* (September 9, 2024), https://educationdata.org/average-cost-of-college-by-year (accessed 08-04-2025).

91 Daniel A. Austin, "The Indentured Generation: Bankruptcy and Student Loan Debt," *The Santa Clara Law Review* (August 22, 2013), Volume 52, Number 1, Article 1, p. 410.

92 Harzog, *Confessions*, p. 99.

93 Austin, "Indentured Generation," *The Santa Clara Law Review*, p. 401.

94 Ibid., p. 388.

95 Terry Golway (ed.), *American Political Speeches* (New York: Penguin, 2012), p. xxvi-xxviii and pp. 1-3; Bruce Borland and Jessica Bayne, *America Through the Eyes of its People* (New York: Longman, 1997), pp. 21-23; and Arthur M. Schlesinger. Jr., *The Cycles of American History* (Boston: Houghton Mifflin, 1986), p. 15.

96 Andro Linklater, *Measuring America: How an Untamed Wilderness Shaped the United States and Fulfilled the Promise of Democracy* (New York: Walker, 2002), p. 27.

97 "Incarceration Rates in Selected Countries," Statista *Research Department* (February 20, 2025) *http://statista.com/statistics/262962/countries-with-the-most-prisoners-per-100-000-inhabitants/* (accessed 04-12-2025).

98 See The Federal Trade *Commission's Consumer Sentinel Network: Law Enforcement's Source for Consumer Complaints: Top 50 Companies Receiving Consumer Sentinel Network Complaints* (May 1, 2023 thru May 31, 2023) https://www.ftc.gov/system/files/ftc_gov/pdf/top_co_complaints_may_2023.pdf and "Justice Department and Consumer Financial Protection Bureau Reach $169 Million Settlement to Resolve Allegations of Credit Card Lending Discrimination by GE Capital Retail Bank," *Archives: U.S. Department of Justice* (June 14, 2014) *https://www.justice.gov/archives/opa/pr/justice-department-and-consumer-finan-cial-protection-bureau-reach-169-million-settlement* (both accessed 04-24-2025).

99 Paul Myer Mazur, a Wall Street banker and who eventually rose to be a senior partner of Lehman Brothers, wrote in his 1927 business textbook, *Principles of Organization Applied to Modern Retailing*, that contained his approach to promoting consumer products. See Leach, Land of Desire, pp. 285-286.

100 Christine Ammer, *The American Heritage Dictionary of Idioms* (New York: Houghton Mifflin Harcourt, 2013), p. 251.

101 See Leach, Land of Desire, p. 7 and p. 16 and Watts, *Citizen Cowboy*, p. 311.

102 *Why eight months?* Orman elaborated in her consumer advice book that "well, it's not just because 4 in 10 people who are unemployed today have been out of work for more than six months. . . . there are less dramatic and more frequent emergencies that happen throughout the course of any given year. Your car may need new brakes. Your water heater may go on the fritz. Your kid tears a ligament

playing soccer and suddenly you have $1,000 in copays for the doctor bills." Suze Orman, *The Money Class: Learn to Create Your Own American Dream* (New York: Spiegel and Grau, 2011), p. 23.

[103] Thomas J. Stanley and William D. Danko, *The Millionaire Next Door: The Surprising Secrets of America's Wealthy* (Lanham, MD: Taylor Trade Publishing, 1996), p. 27 and p. 29.

[104] Alice Schroeder, *The Snowball: Warren Buffett and the Business of Life* (New York: Bantam, 2008), p. 653.

[105] Dave Ramsey, *Million Dollar Makeover: A Proven Plan for Financial Peace—the Expanded and Updated Edition* (Nashville: Nelson Books, 2024), p. xv.

BIBLIOGRAPHY

Archival Sources

Proclamation of the 1825 Treaty of Doak Stand between the United States of America and the Choctaw (7 Stat., 234), promulgated on February 19, 1825.

Electronic Sources

Bram, Jason and Sydney Ludvigson, "Does Consumer Confidence Forecast Household Expenditure? A Sentiment Index Horse Race," *Federal Reserve Bank of New York*, https://www.google.com/search?q=criticisms+of+consumer+confidence+indices&rlz=1C1GCEA_enUS1133US1133&oq=criticisms+of+consumer+confidence+indces+&gs_lcrp=EgZjaHJvbWUqBggBECEYCjIGCAAQRRg-5MgYIARAhGAoyBwgCECEYjwIyBwgDECEYjwLSAQkzMTMzN2owajSoAg-CwAgE&sourceid=chrome&ie=UTF-8 (accessed 12-04-2025).

Carpenter, David H., Edward V. Murphy, and Maureen M. Murphy, "The Glass-Steagall Act: A Legal and Policy Analysis, *Congress.gov* (January 19, 2016) https://www.congress.gov/crs-product/R44349 (accessed 14-10-2025).

Caruthers, Bruce G, Timothy W. Guinnane, and Yoonseok Lee, "The Passage of the Uniform Small Loan Law," *Internet Archive* (January 2007), https://web.archive.org/web/20150923203136/http://www.cgdev.org/doc/blog/Roodman%20open%20book/Caruthers,%20Guinnane,%20and%20Lee,%20The%20Passage %20of%20the%20Uniform%20Small%20Loan%20Law.pdf. (accessed 16-02-25).

"Countries with the Highest National Debt 2025," *World Population Review* https://worldpopulationreview.com/country-rankings/countries-by-national-debt (accessed 03-21-2025).

"COVID-19: Household Debt During the Pandemic," *Congress.gov*, https://www.congress.gov/crsproduct/R46578#:~:text=Mortgage%20debt%20increased%2C%20and%20other,the%202007%2D2009%20Great%20Recession (accessed 05-04-25).

"Current Federal Debt and Deficit," *Peter G. Peterson Foundation*, https://www.pgpf.org/programs-and-projects/fiscal-policy/current-debt-deficit/ (accessed 03-21-2025).

The Federal Trade Commission's Consumer Sentinel Network: Law Enforcement's Source for Consumer Complaints: Top 50 Companies Receiving Consumer Sentinel Network Complaints (May 1, 2023 thru May 31, 2023),

https://www.ftc.gov/system/files/ftc_gov/pdf/top_co_complaints_may_2023.pdf and "Justice Department and Consumer Financial Protection Bureau Reach $169 Million Settlement to Resolve Allegations of Credit Card Lending Discrimination by GE Capital Retail Bank," *Archives: U.S. Department of Justice* (June 14, 2014) https://www.justice.gov/archives/opa/pr/justice-department-and-consumer-financial-protection-bureau- reach-169-million-settlement (both accessed 04-24-2025).

Hanson, Melanie, "Average Cost of College by Year," The Education Data Initiative (September 9, 2024), https://educationdata.org/average-cost-of-college-by-year (accessed 08-04-2025).

Ana Hernández, Anna and Lowell R. Ricketts, "The State of U.S. Wealth Inequality," *Federal Reserve Bank of St. Louis* (October 22, 2024), https://www.stlouisfed.org/community-development-research/the-state-of-us-wealth-inequality (accessed 24-02-2025).

Hoofnagle, Chris Jay, "The FTC's Historical–and Enduring–Challenges," *Chris Hoofnagle: UC Berkeley School of Law*, http://www.law360.com/privacy/articles/753384/ftc-s-early-consumer-protection-challenges-endure   (accessed 10-03-2025).

Horowitz, Alex, "Economic Mobility and Family Finances," *Consumer Finance* (June 2, 2023) https://www.pewtrusts.org/en/research-and--analysis/articles/2023/06/02/payday-loans-and-overdraft-a-short-history-and-whats next#:~:text=Modern%20payday%20loans%20emerged% 20in,in%20more%20than%20 30%20states (accessed 16-02-25).

Howe, Amy, "Supreme Court Strikes Down Biden Student-Loan Forgiveness Program," *SCOTUS Blog Independent News and Analysis of the U.S. Supreme Court*, (June 30, 2023) https://www.scotusblog.com/2023/06/supreme-court-strikes-down-biden-student-loan-forgiveness-program/ (accessed 08-05-2025).

"Incarceration Rates in Selected Countries," *Statista Research Department* (February 20, 2025), http://statista.com/statistics/262962/countries-with-the-most-prisoners-per-100-000-inhabitants/ (accessed 04-12-2025).

Lubove, Seth, "After 37 Years, Billionaire Ford Still Eager to Flip Banks for Profit," *The Standard Times: South Coast Today* (August 19, 2012), https://www.southcoasttoday.com/story/business/2012/0 8/19/after-37-years-billionaire-ford/49460472007/ (accessed 22-04-2025).

Myers, Zach, "More Americans under Credit Card Stress," *FOX59 News—Nexstar Media Inc.*, (February 3, 2025) https://fox59.com/news/more-americans-under-under- credit-card-stress/ (accessed 03-21-2025).

Quinn, Gene and Steve Brachmann, "Mark Twain: Celebrated American Novelist, Inventor and Champion of a Strong Patent System," *IPA Watchdog* (December 16. 2016). https://ipwatchdog.com/2016/12/18/mark-twain-novelist-inventor-champion-patent-system/id=75688/ (accessed 27-02-2025).

"When a Quote is Not (Exactly) a Quote: The Business of America is Business," Edition Library of Congress Blogs: *INSIDE ADAMS Science, Technology, and Business* (ISSN 2691-3690), https://blogs.loc.gov/inside_adams/2019/01/when-a-quote-is-not-exactly-a-quote-the-business-of-america-is-business-edition/ (accessed 05-03-2025).

Books and Compilations

Ammer, Christine. *The American Heritage Dictionary of Idioms*. New York: Houghton Mifflin Harcourt, 2013.

Ammon, Henry. *James Monroe: The Quest for National Identity*. New York: McGraw-Hill, 1971.

Bonner, William and Addison Wiggen, *Empire of Debt: The Rise of an Epic Financial Crisis*. John Wiley & Sons, 2006.

Borland, Bruce and Jessica Bayne, *America Through the Eyes of its People*. New York: Longman, 1997.

Bottela, Elena. *Delinquent: Inside America's Debt Machine*. Oakland: University of California Press, 2022.

Calhoun, Charles W. The Presidency of Ulysses S. Grant. Lawrence: University of Kansas Press, 2017.

Chapman, John H. and associates. "Commercial Bank and Consumer Instalment [sic] Credit" in *The Rise of Consumer Financing by Commercial Banks*. Ann Arbor, MI: National Bureau of Economic Research, 1940.

Chernow, Ron. *Mark Twain*. New York: Penguin, 2025.

Ellis, Joseph J. *American Sphinx: The Character of Thomas Jefferson*. New York: Knopf, 1997.

Ferrell, Robert H. *Harry S. Truman: A Life*. Columbia: University of Missouri Press, 1994.

Gerhardt, Michael. *Lincoln's Mentors: The Education of a Leader*. New York: HarperCollins, 2021.

Golway, Terry, Editor. *American Political Speeches*. New York: Penguin, 2012.

Goodwin, Doris Kearns. *Lyndon Johnson and the American Dream*. New York: St. Martin's Griffin, 1991.

Harzog, Beverly. *Confessions of a Credit Junkie: Everything You Need to Know to Avoid the Mistakes I Made*. Pompton Plains, NJ: Career Press, 2014.

Hyman, Louis. *Debtor Nation: A History of America in Red Ink*. Princeton: Princeton University Press, 2011

Isenberg, Nancy. *Fallen Founder: The Life of Aaron Burr*. New York: Viking, 2007.

Keneally, Thomas. *Abraham Lincoln: A Life*. New York: Penguin, 2008.

Kieman, Denise and Joseph D'Agnese. *Signing Their Lives Away: The Fame and Misfortune of the Men who Signed the Declaration of Independence*. Philadelphia: Quirk Books, 2019.

Lauer, John. *Creditworthy: A History of Consumer Surveillance and Financial Identity in America*. New York: Columbia University Press, 2017.

Leach, William. *Land of Desire: Merchants, Power, and the Rise of a New American Culture*. New York: Pantheon Books, 1993.

Lepore, Jill. *These Truths: A History of the United States*. New York: W. W. Norton, 2018.

Linklater, Andro. *Measuring America: How an Untamed Wilderness Shaped the United States and Fulfilled the Promise of Democracy*. New York: Walker, 2002.

Madsen, Axel. *John Jacob Astor: America's First Multimillionaire*. New York: Wiley & Sons, 2001.

Maier, Pauline, Merritt Roe Smith, Alexander Keyssar, and Daniel Kevles. *Inventing America*. New York: W. W. Norton, 2003.

McCullough, David. Truman. New York: Touchstone, 1992.

McGrath, Tim. *James Monroe: A Life*. New York: Dutton, 2020.

Meacham, Jon. And There Was Light: *Abraham Lincoln and the American Struggle*. New York: Random House, 2022.

Meltzer, Milton, *Edgar Allan Poe: A Biography*. Brookfield, CT: Twenty-First Century Books, 2003.

Mintzberg, Henry, Editor. *Mintzberg on Management*. New York: The Free Press 1989.

Orman, Suze. *The Money Class: Learn to Create Your Own American Dream*. New York: Spiegel and Grau, 2011.

Ramsey, Dave. *Million Dollar Makeover: A Proven Plan for Financial Peace*. Nashville: Nelson Books [the Expanded and Updated Edition], 2024.

Rothschild, Mike. *Jewish Space Lasers: The Rothschilds and 200 Years of Conspiracy Theories*. Brooklyn: Melville House, 2023.

Shulman, Seth. The Telephone Gambit: Chasing Alexander Graham Bell's Secret. New York: W. W. Norton, 2008.

Schlesinger. Jr., Arthur M. *The Cycles of American History*. (Boston: Houghton Mifflin, 1986.

Schroeder, Alice. *The Snowball: Warren Buffett and the Business of Life*. New York: Bantam, 2008.

See, Harold F, "Bankruptcy," *The Encyclopedia of the United States Congress*. New York: Simon & Schuster, 1995. Volume I, p. 145.

Stanley, Thomas J. and William D. Danko. *The Millionaire Next Door: The Surprising Secrets of America's Wealthy*. Lanham, MD: Taylor Trade Publishing, 1996.

Stephens, John Richard. *Gold: Firsthand Accounts from the Rush that Made the West*. Guilford, CT: Twodot, 2014.

Takaki, Ronald. *A Different Mirror: A History of Multicultural America* (New York: Back Bay, 2008.

de Tocqueville, Alexis. *Democracy in America*. Translated by Arthur Goldhammer. New York: Library of America, 2004. Volume Two, Part III, Chapter 18.

Veblen, Thorstein. *The Theory of the Leisure Class: An Economic Study of Institutions*. New York: Modern Library, 1934 [1899].

Wallis, Michael. *David Crockett: "Lion of the West."* New York: W. W. Norton, 2011.

Watts, Steven. *Citizen Cowboy: Will Rogers and the American People*. New York: Cambridge University Press, 2024.

White, Richard. *The Republic for Which It Stands: The United States during Reconstruction and the Gilded Age, 1865-1896*. New York: Oxford University Press, 2017.

Zunz, Olivier. *The Man Who Understood Democracy: The Life of Alexis de Tocqueville*. Princeton: Princeton University Press, 2022.

Articles

Austin, Daniel A, "The Indentured Generation: Bankruptcy and Student Loan Debt," *The Santa Clara Law Review* (August 22, 2013), Volume 52, Number 1, Article 1, pp. 410-411.

"Credit Cards: A Push to Cap Interest at 10 Percent," *The Week: The Best of the U.S. and International Media* (February 21, 2025), p. 33.

Dilworth, Kelly, "Your Money: The Rising Costs of Using a Credit Card," *AARP Bulletin* (January-February 2025), pp. 20-21.

Index

Page numbers for illustrations appear in italics; those for endnotes include the number of the endnote following the abbreviation *n* (e.g., 149*n*5).

About the Author

DANIEL PATRICK BROWN is a professor and academic dean emeritus from Moorpark College (CA). Professor Brown has authored several historical works, including *The Beautiful Beast Life & Crimes of SS-Aufseherin Irma Grese* (2004) and *American Chronicle: An Inclusive History*, Volume I (2024). He was named the Moorpark College Distinguished Faculty Chair recipient in 1996, and he has also served as an interviewer for the "Survivors of the Shoah Visual History Project."

www.ingramcontent.com/pod-product-compliance
Lightning Source LLC
LaVergne TN
LVHW051247080426
835513LV00016B/1784